God's Church in the World

God's Church in the World

The Gift of Catholic Mission

Edited by Susan Lucas

On behalf of Anglican Catholic Future
and Forward in Faith

CANTERBURY
PRESS
Norwich

Published in 2020 by Canterbury Press
Editorial office
3rd Floor, Invicta House,
108–114 Golden Lane,
London EC1Y OTG, UK
www.canterburypress.co.uk

Canterbury Press is an imprint of Hymns Ancient & Modern Ltd
(a registered charity)

Hymns Ancient & Modern® is a registered trademark of
Hymns Ancient & Modern Ltd
13A Hellesdon Park Road, Norwich,
Norfolk NR6 5DR, UK

Unless otherwise stated, Scripture quotations are from New Revised
Standard Version Bible: Anglicized Edition, copyright © 1989, 1995
National Council of the Churches of Christ in the United States of
America. Used by permission. All rights reserved worldwide.

British Library Cataloguing in Publication data

A catalogue record for this book is available
from the British Library

978 1 78622 240 4

Typeset by Regent Typesetting
Printed and bound by
CPI Group (UK) Ltd

Contents

v

Part 3 Reflections on Scripture

Part 4 Catholic Mission in Historical Perspective

Acknowledgements

This book, and the conference at which most of the papers in these chapters were originally given, has been a collaborative enterprise from the beginning; so, while I have pulled the manuscript together on behalf of Anglican Catholic Future and Forward in Faith, neither conference nor book would have happened without the organizing committee of the conference – namely, Peter Anthony, Ian McCormack and Ross Northing of Forward in Faith; and Imogen Black, Michael Bowie and Christopher Woods of Anglican Catholic Future. I should also like to thank Colin Podmore for his wise counsel at various points in both the organization of the conference and production of the book. Last but not least, I would like to thank my family, Tony Lucas, Joe Lucas and Joyce Morris, for their support in this and in much else.

Introduction

This is a book that began with intentional, if improbable, friendship, in the determination of a group of faithful Catholic Anglicans, united in their devotion to Catholic piety and practice, and to the parish as the Anglican way of being God's Church in the world, but divided by their views on the ordained ministry of women, to 'reach across the aisle' for the sake of the mission of the Church. The project began in May 2016, in a joint retreat for equal numbers of representatives of Forward in Faith and Anglican Catholic Future. As we talked together, laughed together, argued, prayed, ate and drank together and received Christ in the Eucharist, we discovered much common ground. In particular, there was a shared sense that the Catholic tradition of the Church of England is missional *ab initio*, formed by a conviction that the presence of Christ in the Eucharist intensifies and motivates an awareness of the sacramental presence of Christ in the world – God's Church in God's world exists for the sake of the *Missio Dei*, the sending of the loving God into his creation in the Son, and its continuation, through the Holy Spirit, in the life of the Church. A smaller group within the main group was formed to become the organizing committee for a conference, held at Lambeth Palace, St Andrew Holborn, and St Dunstan-in-the-West in September 2018.

The chapters in the book were originally papers from, and reflections on, that conference. As the steering group worked together and the conference got under way, trust increased, friendships deepened, and hope was renewed. This book is now offered to widen the conversation, extend the hand of friendship in the Catholic tradition of the Church of England and beyond it, in the hope that our sisters and brothers in Christ discover riches in Anglican Catholic piety and practice that are offered as gifts to the wider Church in its task of participating faithfully and fully in the mission of God.

The last decade and a half, since the publication of *Mission-shaped Church* (Mission-shaped Church Working Group, 2004), has seen an increased emphasis on mission in the Church of England. Much of this has been driven by, and uses the language of, evangelical Christianity and identifies mission closely with evangelism. At one level, this is right and proper; however, those of a Catholic tradition have sometimes felt at odds with the language and presuppositions of this movement. The conference sought to articulate positively what is distinctive about a Catholic understanding of mission, in a language in which Catholics of all 'tribes' in the Church of England would feel at home, yet in an inclusive and generous way, seeking to converse with others. Several key themes, neither exclusive nor exhaustive, but characteristic of Catholic mission, emerged in a number of different ways in the conference papers, and are reflected in what follows. They are: a sense that mission needs to be church-shaped, as well as Church being mission-shaped; the essentially missional nature of worship, particularly sacramental worship, and the sense that the sacraments are themselves missional; the importance for Catholic mission of a generous, inclusive and robust theological anthropology; an emphasis on the importance of place and appropriate limits, as opposed to narratives of unlimited growth; the generosity of God. The conference also named several tensions within Catholic understandings of mission, and between them and the wider Church: one is a non-instrumental view of mission as an invitation to be caught up in the life of the Church, over against the language of strategy, leadership and management; and, within the Catholic tradition itself, a tension about the proper role of women, and particularly of working-class women in leadership and mission in the Church, a tension that exists no less for those able to accept the ordained ministry of women than for those who do not.

One corrective, then, to the language and presuppositions of evangelical understandings of mission that emerge from what follows is that it is not just 'mission-shaped Church', but also 'Church-shaped mission'. That is, mission is never simply about drawing the individual believer into relationship with Jesus Christ, an account of mission in which the Church is understood almost incidentally, and rather instrumentally. The Church, the living body of Christ, nourished on the sacraments and the sacramental word of Scripture, is involved necessarily with mission, since mission is always and essentially corporate, the activity of the living body of Christ that is sent out in order that more might be drawn into its life.

Rowan Williams draws attention to this in Chapter 1, pointing out the essential link between mission and prayer, thus 'nurturing the deepest connection within the body of Christ, in which the eternal life of the world is made available'; the Church being 'the eternal happening of the world's adoration [of God] here and now'. From a different perspective, Anna Matthews makes a similar point in Chapter 5: in reflecting on vocation, the question of what priests are for immediately begs the question of what the Church is for, and that takes us into the territory of mission.

Several writers in the book emphasize the centrality of worship to mission, and in particular, of the sacraments, bringing the grace of conversion into the lives of individuals and communities. Proclamation is at its most powerful when it is rooted in the sacraments, which, as Andrew Davison puts it in Chapter 9, is not a question of more spiritual, less physical, more word, less sacrament, more God, less humanity, but a holistic vision in which the physical, the spiritual, God and humanity are all present in the sacramental life of the Church, which is at the same time the proclamation of the joy and hope of the gospel. On this view, it is axiomatic that worship is missional – the encounter with Christ in the sacrament is the springboard by which the believer is sent out to witness to the joyful truth of the gospel by acts of loving service and challenge to injustice.

A further theme evident in several of the chapters is that of the centrality of humanity to mission. Thus, in Chapter 2 Alison Milbank emphasizes that mission is trinitarian, and that in mission, humanity is drawn into the body of Christ, the Church, and therefore also into the life of the divine society that is the Trinity. Mission is thus a gift, the gift of a human life, one that has a particular shape, with its own teleology, and also its own distinctive challenges. An aspect of this shape of life is also social justice, since being drawn into the life of the divine society raises questions about what it means to be human, and in particular what it means to be human together, to be called into the social sphere and therefore also into justice.

There is also, in several writers' chapters, an emphasis on the sacramental importance of place in mission. In an age of so-called 'somewheres' and 'anywheres' (see Goodhart, 2017), a distinction that itself deserves more refinement and nuance than it has sometimes been given, those concerned with Catholic mission provide some refinement and nuance in affirming a crucial aspect of the parish system – that is, its focus on the particular and the *placed*. To do so is sacramental, since, as Rowan Williams has argued elsewhere, to take the sacraments seriously is to 'learn to live in a material world without resentment' (Williams, 2007, p. 186). That 'without resentment' – that generosity – is about clear-eyed recognition not of scarcity but of limit; of, as the psalmist has it, 'boundaries in pleasant places' (Ps. 16.6). In terms of mission, it is recognizing there is a limit both to the numbers we can reach, but also of their 'givenness'. As one parish priest once put it to me, '*These* are the people God has given us to love.' Part of the tension between this and some evangelical understandings of mission is in the apparent resistance of the latter to the very idea of the parish. But this is often at cross purposes: what is often and rightly critiqued is a model of one priest, one parish – sometimes caricatured as 'one pope, one parish'. In fact, as a model of parish life, this is only as old as the late nineteenth century and, as Stephen Spencer points out in Chapter 10, was critiqued from a Catholic perspective by the Tractarian method of founding communities to work in mission in parishes. What needs to be affirmed, and is, for example by the diocese of Chelmsford's Transforming Presence Agenda (2011), is the rich possibilities provided by the limits of place, which is both arbitrary and specific – in the parish system, there is no place that is not someone's cure of souls, and every place is a place for which it is somebody's responsibility to pray.

Andrew Davison, in particular, emphasizes in Chapter 9 the importance in Catholic mission of recognizing the generosity of God; in a world of strategy and agendas, in Sam Wells's memorable words, 'God gives his people everything they need to worship him, to be his friends and to eat with him' (Wells, 2006, p. 1). Generosity that is invitational to gratitude and sharing is a lovely image, in Davison's words, of the Church as the 'boat' in which the fearful disciples come to see the power of God's generosity.

A Catholic understanding of mission, then, as it emerges in what follows, is church-shaped and corporate, has worship, and the sacraments in particular, at its heart; as trinitarian, it draws people into the life of a divine society, is shaped by the specificity and arbitrariness of place as 'boundaries in pleasant places', and by a rich understanding of the Church as the boat in which the fearful experience God's generosity. There are undoubted tensions between this understanding of mission and evangelical understandings which, as we saw earlier, emphasize a highly personal and individual encounter with Jesus, an encounter to which the Church is incidental and instrumental. In Chapter 6 Damian Feeney both names this tension and also points hopefully to it being a creative tension.

Conversation about the nature of evangelism is prone to displacement discussions about strategy, models and case studies (see p. 86), but Feeney sees hope in that the trajectory of such displacement activity is in the ultimate recognition that it is God who is the evangelist. Luke Miller provides a good example in Chapter 3 of how to inhabit this dialectical tension creatively, giving proper place to the best that can be learned from strategy, models and case studies, while at the same time insisting that mission is rooted in personal spiritual growth and holiness, disciplined private devotion, and the recognition that the one soul a person can really hope to convert is their own. Therefore, used carefully and thoughtfully, strategy need not be exhausted by the instrumental.

A further tension, one this time within Catholic understandings of mission, is that between the 'two integrities' within the Catholic tradition of the Church of England, a nail that Philip North, in Chapter 4, hits squarely on the head:

> ... our failure to identify the central role that women, and especially women from poorer backgrounds, should be occupying in the Church's life. Those who accept the ordination of women think the issue is solved when it isn't (especially when our processes of vocational discernment structurally eliminate the poor). Those who cannot accept the ordination of women, but who still see the ministry and leadership of women as integral to the Church's life, are yet to give adequately imaginative answers to how those two viewpoints are reconciled. (p. 64)

Philip North is surely right to identify both that the central role that women should play in the Church is not settled simply by the ordination of women – and, in particular, the absence of working-class women from orders demonstrates that our vocational processes do indeed favour white, educated middle-class women (and men) – and that those who cannot in conscience accept the ordination of women but still see women's ministry and leadership as central to the life of the Church have yet to give a really imaginative positive account as to how that circle is to be squared. He is also surely right to link this tension with some of the 'still weeping wounds of the Reformation'. In being named, this tension ceased to be the 'elephant in the room' at the conference. Naming is not, in itself, a means of resolving the tension, but it is a start at recognizing it as potentially creative and, perhaps, for both constituencies an opportunity to repent that our past battles have compromised the full flourishing of mission in the Catholic tradition of the Church of England.

If the Church of God – not just the Church of England – is to be truly 'mission-shaped', then it needs this Catholic perspective, with its emphasis on the corporate, sacramental and the whole people of God. How, then, can Anglican Catholics (re) discover a language that enables them really to be missional, to engage fully with a mission-shaped Church not just without resentment, but giving it an honoured place in the body of Christ, complementary to the undoubted good work done by evangelicals? This book, and the conference that inspired it, explores this question from a number of angles.

In Part 1 of the book, Rowan Williams argues that mission begins in the life of prayer (Chapter 1). He reminds us of the conviction of Catholics that the Church *is* because God *is*, and God acts – and that, therefore, however difficult it is in times like ours, and however many things we might be anxious about, there is no need to be anxious about the Church's future. Rowan's chapter contains the first expression in this book of the central thought that mission is not a recruitment policy or publicity campaign, but a means of extending an invitation into the life of God, and into the life of God's new creation both now and in eternity, an invitation that comes with an immediate challenge to 'take up one's cross'; the sacramental practice of the Church shows the shape of that life, both the invitation and the challenge.

Alison Milbank, in Chapter 2, argues that the Catholic tradition conceives of the Church as a human society or community, founded on the life of the Trinity, in which 'our worship bears witness to God's holiness and the call to become holy' (p. 20). Catholic mission, then, is in a benign sense holistic, 'according to the whole', and is at the same time distinctive, in being embodied, incarnational, often radically concerned with social justice, scripturally rooted, and able to occupy a distinctive, liminal space between the Church and the wider culture that is sometimes affirming and sometimes critical.

In Chapter 3, and building on this conception of mission as rooted in the life of the Trinity, Luke Miller argues that, in practice, church growth actually begins with personal growth in holiness. He approvingly quotes the Cowley Father George Congreve, that the one soul whose conversion I must be responsible for is my own; growth in depth of faith, of personal holiness, leads to growth in numbers; Catholic practice, 'being busy about the sacraments; personal prayer; confession; catechesis; habits of holiness; the consecration of home life by simple things', represents a response to the 'fact that "Christ has taken human nature and made all one"' (p. 37). All of this represents a language in which we can speak in the public sphere to share the joy and hope of the gospel, and which can have an effect on the Church's growth in numbers in appropriately measurable ways. As Miller says, we measure what we value in order not to value what we measure – and we measure what is measurable so that the immeasurable love of God might be known. Miller recognizes the holistic nature of mission that the first two chapters of Part 1 rightly insist upon, and its connection with worship and the sacramental life; he begins to address head-on the dialectical tension between this conception of mission and the language of strategy, targets and statistics, and how such a conception of mission can, with integrity, engage with that language.

Part 2 of the book, based on seminars on the middle day of the conference, consists of conversations on various aspects of these themes. So, in Chapter 4, Philip North and Gemma Simmonds suggest that devotion to the Blessed Virgin Mary, far from being inward, private and rather esoteric, represents radical engagement with the everyday, and most particularly with those at the margins of society.

In Chapter 5, Anna Matthews and Robin Ward argue that the Catholic tradition, with a commitment to the whole body of Christ (from the Greek *kata-holon*), has always promoted the vocations of all the baptized – and given an honoured place to lay ministry in ways that the wider Church is only just beginning to rediscover. Matthews rightly recognizes that questions of vocation immediately lead us into questions of what the Church is for, and hence into the nature of mission. Her answer is that the Church is a 'priestly people' – and therefore mission is enabling others to hear the call to belong to such a community, in which is healing, reconciliation, growth and holiness, anticipating here and now the reconciliation of all things in Christ. Priests who can learn to be at home in the landscape of the new creation are missional priests. Robin Ward suggests that to be Catholic is not to belong to a party, but is about being the Church. The *objective* ground of mission is the worship of God; its *subjective* ground is the whole undertaking of Christian practice that flows from liturgical life.

Social justice has been central to Catholic mission in the Church of England since the days of the Oxford Movement. In Chapter 7 Simon Morris identifies the importance of the parish as central to this – the 'fourth mark of mission'. The parish is the place in which we discover what it means to be human and, in particular, what it means to be human together. In the same chapter, Ric Thorpe also recognizes the importance of parish as being both 'in place' and well placed to find common ground in accounts of mission between Catholics and evangelicals, since it is the locus of proclamation through seeking to come alongside those on the margins and to help in practical ways. He directly connects church planting with evangelization and social justice, since, as new people become embedded in the community, God calls them to learn from it, to love it, and to be transformed and transforming: 'it is the whole Church [Catholic], in all its traditions and tribes, that God calls to love and transform his world' (p. 109).

Anna Matthews (Chapter 8) and Andrew Davison (Chapter 9) offer some reflections on Scripture in relation to mission-shaped Catholic piety in pieces that began life as sermons at

Mass and Evensong in the conference, while in Chapter 10 Stephen Spencer, Director for Theological Education in the Anglican Communion (who was not present at the Conference), offers a wider perspective on Catholic mission in a historical perspective.

United by a desire to inspire and equip both clergy and laity for the work of Christian mission rooted in Catholic practice, piety and theology, without recourse to political agendas and rivalries, the chapters in this volume are offered in generosity – a generosity that has been so palpably present throughout the process that led both to the conference and to the production of this book. The same generosity is present in the Five Guiding Principles that provide the means whereby those of different integrities in the Church of England can mutually recognize one another and mutually flourish. That mutual flourishing is modelled in this book, and if the sense of the nature of mission that emerges from it is of mission as rooted in the life of the Trinity – shaped by being formed in personal holiness, incarnational and committed to social justice, enabling a renewed 'scriptural imaginary' and as local, specific and contextual – then it is our hope that it is one small way in which the form of those guiding principles is given content, and in which the mutual flourishing they outline might be made flesh.

Bibliography

Diocese of Chelmsford (2011), *Transforming Presence*, online at www. chelmsford.anglican.org/uploads/TransformingPresence.pdf.

Goodhart, David (2017), *The Road to Somewhere: The Populist Revolt and the Future of Politics*, London: C. Hurst and Co.

Mission-shaped Church Working Group (2004), *Mission-shaped Church: Church Planting and Fresh Expressions in a Changing Context*, London: Church House Publishing.

Wells, Samuel (2006), *God's Companions: Reimagining Christian Ethics*, Oxford: Blackwell.

Williams, Rowan (2007), 'The Suspicion of Suspicion', in Mike Higton (ed.), *Wrestling with Angels*, London: SCM Press, pp. 186–202.

PART I

Themes

I

Mission and the Life of Prayer

ROWAN WILLIAMS

In our Church at the moment there is, if not exactly a struggle, certainly a tension about how we imagine the Church itself. If we are going to speak about prayer in the context of the Church's mission, it seems to me that we need to begin by framing our discussion very clearly in relation to the conviction that we share as Catholic Christians: that the Church *is* because God *is* and acts, not because of what we do or we think. We did not invent the Church. The Church, the body of Christ, is given to us as the means of our participation in an eternal reality, which, as St Augustine unforgettably said, 'does not fall down because we happen to be out of doors'. So that's the context within which I want to talk about prayer in relation to mission. We believe that we do not need, strange as that may sound, to be anxious about the Church's future. We may be anxious about *our* future. We may be anxious about paying quotas, filling parishes. We may even be anxious about the statistics of recent opinion polls concerning the Church of England in the life of the nation; but what we do *not* need to be anxious about is the Church. It is because God is and God acts. So to engage in mission is not to engage in a recruitment or publicity campaign. It is to seek day after day to extend the invitation built into God's very being, the invitation to creation to share God's very life, and that's why, in a nutshell, prayer matters.

Within that overall framework, let me begin to think with you a little bit about prayer itself, with words from one of our greatest Anglican theologians, George Herbert. His sonnet on prayer begins:

Prayer, the Church's banquet, angels' age,
God's breath in man returning to his birth.

It's that theme of God's breath in us returning to where it came from that I want to treat as the cornerstone of what we might think and say about prayer.

In the early nineteenth century, Samuel Taylor Coleridge, in his literary essays, defined imagination as 'a repetition in time of the eternal I am'; and I want to suggest that what Coleridge says about the imagination is what we ought to be saying about prayer. It is the repetition of God in us; the repetition in time of the eternal I am. The eternal reality that prayer repeats and makes visible in our history is the eternal fact of the life of the Word of God; a life that is exposed to, and adoring of, God the Father, without qualification, without interruption. That eternal exposure to and adoration of the divine source of being, which is the life of the Word, is what is most real. The reality of creation itself exists because of that. All things were made through him, or by him, or in him. In the Word all things have their root and their ground, and if the Word, in whom all things have their root and their ground, is exposure and adoration, then that is itself the most real of all realities. In so far as we can define prayer as exposure to God and adoration of God, prayer is that in which and on which all things subsist. To put it another way, prayer in that sense is quite simply what's 'happening'; not what's happening anywhere in particular, just what's *happening* – the eternal giving of God, the gift of the Father and the loving adoration of the Son and the outpouring of the Spirit is what is happening, full stop. If that is what's going on under the surface of all our action, speech and reflection, then we can perhaps see why we need not fear. There is something about the life of prayer understood in these terms that is fundamentally about not being afraid. We badly need to build that into our own self-understanding as a believing people, and into our own understanding of what it is we seek to share with the world around, where being afraid is something of a default setting for a great deal of the human race, for a variety of reasons, good and bad.

I've gone back many times to a little book on prayer written in the 1970s by the Dominican Simon Tugwell, in which he says that the Hebrew word for 'trusting in God' or 'relying on God', which we are encouraged to do in prayer, is the same as the word 'to lie back upon'; lie back upon God, rest upon what is happening. And so prayer, in this context, is the act, the eternal act, that we live in and live from, not a transaction that we initiate. It is not a long and laborious journey to a distant distribution office. It is not a troubled and fearful attempt to win points from an eternal scorekeeper. It is already what we live from, beyond and before anything we do or are or understand; and so to try and nurture God's people in prayer, beginning with ourselves, is first and foremost to nurture a connection with that deepest reality that is the body of Christ in which the eternal life of the Word is made available to us. We need, to put it simply, to be connected with the Church's experience as Church, the Church's sense of itself and conviction about itself as Christ's body; not as the variously muddled, embarrassing, shabby, confused, unsuccessful, blathering reality that we are mostly familiar with, and that we give so much of our energies to in our own blathering and confusion. The Church's experience is being in Christ. In speaking about prayer, to one another and to the people we minister to, we might have to begin by saying, 'remember that it's always first the Church that prays, because it's always first Christ who prays'. So rather than a map on which you place Christ in one place as an inspiring significant figure to whom you hope to relate creatively, and the Church in another place as an institution that helpfully connects you in some rather unspecified way with this distant figure of the inspiring Jesus, and yourself as an individual somewhere else negotiating your way between these points, we need rather to begin with a sense of the eternal happening of the Word's adoration, a pouring of that life into the world's history in the Incarnate Christ and the Spirit released by his life, death and resurrection, and our participation in what arises from and flows from that reality. Christ prays, the Church prays, we pray, I pray, here and now. The Spirit is what creates in us that repetition of the eternal in time that is our prayer, our reflection of the eternal reality. This is spelled out in depth and detail by Paul in chapter 8 of the letter to the Romans, the Spirit praying with our spirit, the Spirit putting into our mouths the words of Christ to his Father, 'Abba'. This suggests two complementary consequences. First, all authentic prayer in the Church is quite simply what leads us deeper into the life of Christ, into our filiation, our status as daughters and sons of the Eternal. Authentic prayer is what leads us deeper into that life. And, second, it is that life into which we are led that constantly makes our prayer possible, that returns us to praying.

Once upon a time I heard somebody say that a very shrewd priest had advised her in the confessional to discover what it felt like to stop praying for a month. Although that's very odd advice indeed, I think that what he meant his penitent to hear was, 'Try to live as if you were holding your breath, or not eating. Try to live at odds with the deepest reality of your baptized life, and you'll see why prayer is not an extra, a duty, something "tacked on" to discipleship.' Prayer simply is the articulation of where and who and what you are, and some-times it is only by the strange exercise of holding back from it that we realize why we miss it. So all authentic prayer takes us deeper into the life of the Word; the life of the Word draws us again and again into prayer.

Now these are somewhat dizzying perspectives on the life of prayer, and they may not immediately feel very real when we blearily open our Office books, or settle ourselves a little reluctantly for another attempt at what a Roman Catholic writer (the novelist Thomas Keneally, in his neglected but still engaging fiction about Australian Catholics in the mid-1960s,

Three Cheers for the Paraclete) once called 'the token assault on the citadel' that you make as you try to open your eyes and ears and heart to God. Yet this immersion in divinity is what is actually happening, whatever we are aware of, whatever we think or imagine about our – dreadful phrase – 'prayer life'. Whatever we think or imagine is happening, what actually 'happens' is the Word and the Spirit and the Father. What happens is the Word's nakedness to and adoration of the Father. It is there already, and our task in prayer is simply to step into it.

Bringing this closer to the practicalities of nourishment in the life of prayer, the most obvious way in is, of course, thanksgiving and adoration – that is to say, reminding ourselves of who God is and what God has done. That's why at one of the key moments in the Mass, what we do is simply spend a moment or so reminding ourselves of who this God is whose action we are celebrating and allowing in; 'Holy, Holy, Holy', we say, having evoked the worship of heaven, as if to say simply, 'We know it's happening'. We know that we are not – as it were – trying to 'confect' it here and now. It is already there. In the Eastern Orthodox liturgies the pre-Sanctus is a wonderfully extravagant statement of just how much is going on: 'We praise God because he is pleased to accept our prayers and praises although there attend upon him thousands of angels, tens of thousands of archangels who, all aloft upon the wing, sing, cry, and shout aloud.'

That's the perspective. That's the happening into which we are inducted. That's why thanksgiving to God for God's glory, the sense of an act that surrounds us, is our primary way in. And Catholic prayer has traditionally focused quite a lot on 'looking': looking into the mystery. Not just looking *at* pretty pictures, but looking *into*. For many, the experience of the adoration of the sacrament is that experience of looking into. After all, what is there to look *at*? A small round wafer and a slightly eccentric piece of miniature architecture. But we look *in*, we look *into* the life of the Word, and that looking, as well as the listening that we do in so many other contexts, is the generative ground of our stepping into this already happening life that is prayer.

Looking into, adoring, giving thanks. This is how it is. Before anything else, Christian worship at its fullest and richest declares quite simply, 'this is how it is'. It doesn't say, 'this is what you should be doing', or 'this is what you should be thinking'. It declares, 'this is what is, this is the real'. What kind of mental and spiritual revolution does it take to persuade us that our worship is an entry into the real; not a kind of 'added extra' to lives of Christian virtue or lives of pious thought, but simply the declaration of what there is? We underrate, I think, the power of *looking* in leading people into prayer. At its fullest, as I've said, we see it in the gaze that we turn on the Blessed Sacrament, but in all kinds of other ways the imagery of the space that surrounds us invites such looking-into, and therefore adoration. And here's a strange thing; equally it's not just the abundance of imagery, it's sometimes the spareness, the spaciousness, even the emptiness, of a place of worship that can induce this looking in. There is, so to speak, a place in the economy of prayer for the equivalent of the Zen garden, as much as for the iconostasis. It's the experience of being taken into that space where we have time and liberty to look, where we don't have to process and output. We can simply see. It's no accident, I think, that one of the great saints of the nineteenth century, the Curé d'Ars, liked to tell the story of the peasant in his parish who spent so much time sitting in front of the Sacrament that when asked by the Curé what he did he simply said, 'je le regarde, et il me regarde'. ('I look at him, and he looks at me'). That is where many people begin – without theory, without elaboration – to discover this entry into the always already reality of prayer.

Having said that, when we are inducted into that place where we have the freedom to look, something else is going on, as the Curé's parishioner knew. 'Il me regarde' – he looks at me. There's an almost imperceptible but crucial moment in understanding our prayer where we, so to speak, tip over from 'I look at' to 'I am being looked at'. I am being looked at; prayer as being where I can be seen by God. I began with two phrases about the everlasting life of the Word, naked to the Father, adoring the Father, receiving the gaze of the Father's eternal love, just as much as pouring out in response the adoration of filial love.

So we begin to move on into a slightly different key of our praying: 'I am looked at' as well as looking. What's involved is not only beholding but being in the light, being in the truth; and this in the experience of so many is of course where adoration, gazing, tips over into repentance. One of the great mistakes we make is to suppose that we always have to begin with penitence. I know there is a traditional logic to how we understand, for example, the flow of the Mass, which quite properly and rightly says we need to say sorry as soon as we can. Fair enough. But thinking generally about prayer, it's not in that first repentance that the energy arises; we don't start with a gaze upon our failure, but a gaze upon the abundance of our God – and in the light of that abundance we discover ourselves. In the light of that beauty we understand why 'beauty' is not always the first thing to be said about our own inner life, or our outer one for that matter! It's out of a commitment to looking into the mystery that there arises that troubling and disturbing element of prayer that obliges us to look into ourselves, knowing that we are seen, knowing that we are seen with *love*, with compassion, with acceptance and with hope, if you can in some way apply that analogically to God – and yet that we are also seen *truthfully*. What God sees when we come before God in prayer, we too must see with God's eyes – that is, to see it clearly, but also to see it in the light of God's mercy.

The moving together of my gaze and God's gaze that happens in prayer – I look at him and he looks at me – and the understanding that somehow I need, as I see myself in repentance, to look at myself in some measure as God looks upon me takes us to a next stage where our prayer involves a kind of imagining of how God sees God's world. God looks at me with creative love, not with disappointment, disgust, sharp intakes of breath and pursed lips. God looks at me with patience, with clarity, and with creative purpose. And if God so looks at me, God so looks at the world. My discovery of myself in penitence before a merciful God opens the door to that alignment with God's seeing of the world and God's purpose for the world that is the ground of our intercession. God sees me clearly and when I see that God sees me, I see myself afresh and begin to allow my self-ignorance, my self-hatred and all the rest to move aside so that God's mercy happens in my heart and in my soul. As that happens, my perspective on the world I inhabit is deepened and enlarged. I draw that little bit closer to wanting what God wants for the creation. That, you could say, is the basis for our thinking about intercession. Intercession, we all know, is not trying to bend God's will to ours, but begins from the conviction that God sees the world with loving purpose and seeks to realize that loving purpose in relation to all the things most deeply and troublingly on our hearts. This is the point where we bring into focus the needs that we are aware of, opening them up as best we can to the divine act that is going on already in relation to these realities.

There are many arguments and discussions that rage around how intercession works, and my normal response to that is to say I have absolutely no idea *how* intercession works and all I know is that I am told to *do* it, and told by a very high authority, so I'd better do it. But in so far as we can begin to understand what is going on, it is surely something to do with this holding before God what is most on my heart, seeking to draw God's loving purpose towards that, and persisting in this imagining of God's purpose in hope. Being ordinary human beings as we are, of course we imagine it in specific form – that is, we pray for particular things; 'let this happen', 'let this healing take place', 'let this reconciliation occur', 'let this person flourish', 'let this conflict be over'. We express our hopes and longings in words – what else could we do? But the act within and beneath those words is simply the act of opening up that situation to the divine loving purpose that we begin to see in ourselves and begin to extend to the whole of God's creation.

Now if in intercession what I'm seeking to do is in that way open up the concerns on my heart and in my mind to God's loving purpose, if what is happening is an attempt to align myself with the will of God, the healing, recreating will of God, that's of course not just an individual act. It's the Church that prays – as we've already noted – and it seems to me of crucial importance that when we think about intercession we think not only about our individual prayer lists, important as they are, essential as they are, but also of our prayer as part of the prayer of an interceding Church. That interceding Church is not simply the Church that listens to the petitions on Sunday morning during Mass. It's the Church that prays in heaven as well as on earth. It's the Church whose entire reality in living in the eternal life of the Word carries God's loving and healing purpose. Just as it's always the whole Church that prays and I within it, so it's the whole Church that intercedes including, thank God, all those souls who have slightly fewer obstacles to their reception of God's will than I do, otherwise known as the saints, who have gone just a few inches beyond what I can even imagine to be possible for myself in their loving alignment with God. We ask the saints to pray with us and for us because they have allowed more of God into their lives and their hearts; it's as simple as that. Their prayer and their presence is an essential element in any action we perform as intercessors, so that what I described as the personal prayer list is something always surrounded by the penumbra of those we ask explicitly and implicitly to pray with us. It's why it is always a good idea to conclude private intercession with the invocation of the Mother of God and the saints. It's why it is important that we explicitly draw the praying life of the Church Triumphant into our own awareness of the needs of others. We pray for one another and with one another. To use that old-fashioned phrase, we pray for one another's 'intentions'; that is, we say in the Church, 'I care about what you care about'. This comes most clearly into focus in our intercession in the Eucharist. In our Anglican liturgies the element of explicit intercession within the Eucharistic Prayer is a bit residual, and our older liturgies and the liturgies of the Christian East preserve the very ancient practice of consciously focusing a major bit of intercession within the Eucharistic Prayer. We could and should learn from this, because this is where the prayer of the Church Militant and Triumphant for the needs of the world most comes into focus.

What I've described so far is a sort of movement from that initial sense of simply being drawn into the mystery to an awareness of our own need and confusion and failure in the face of the mystery, and of the loving purpose that allows us to look at that failure without despair, to an imagining of that loving purpose flowing out, in and through us towards all those for whom we pray. I was taught the old 'ACTS' model of praying – adoration, confession, thanksgiving, supplication; and I had helpful little books that told me what to do for each one. It's seldom as neat as that, though, is it? Yet every element of that mixture matters. And it matters because each element finally leads us back to that fundamental recognition of God's 'breath in us returning to its birth', that fundamental recognition of what is already happening; God's breath returning, the Spirit praying with our spirit.

That process that we enter into in prayer is again and again uncovered for us as the way in which we inhabit the prayer of Christ. To inhabit the prayer of Christ is finally to inhabit the trinitarian life, the exposure to the Father, the adoration of the Son, and the outpouring of life in the Spirit that is the divine act, the divine happening. In the life of the Holy Trinity, so far as we can begin to think about it, the adoration that Christ gives to the Father is not the adoration of one individual for another; instead, it is an absorption and a sharing so unqualified and so profound that some theologians speak of it as the experience of the *non aliud*, the 'not other', 'not another thing', not otherness as we understand it. That's why our prayer, when it matures into the habitual inhabiting of Christ that is contemplation, is characterized by that sense of the *non aliud*, the not other. That's to say that it's not an experience of 'absorption' – what an older generation of scholars in religious studies used to call the 'oceanic experience'; but neither is it simply the experience of talking to somebody on the other side of a room. It's an awareness of the otherness in unity, or something like a heartbeat, or a succession of waves, different and yet the same life configured afresh, responding, echoing, all the time. That's where we are headed, and that is the reality that's the life that we are called in the body of Christ to be a home for in this world.

All this is what's happening as we pray. Prayer is where it happens. At the Mass the life of the Trinity happens in a uniquely intense way, but it happens equally in our variously bored and incompetent attempts to pray in some measure. We must not suppose that our life of prayer is simply like something we undertake for an exam, an activity that we do well or badly. All we can say is, first, that it is a relation to what's always fully there, and second, that its fullness in us is a bit variable depending on our degree of willingness and patience and openness. But being a home for the trinitarian event here in this world also tells us, because our lives are so interconnected, that it's not just about those periods we name as prayerful, it's about the entire work of our life. How do our lives, our bodies, become a home for the trinitarian life? How do we so act in routine daily matters as to keep the door open to the divine life? What are the disciplines that keep us inhabiting the reality, as we inhabit our world, our relationships, our own hopes and fears? It's why it does matter, in spite of all temptations to the contrary, that we think about how we pray with our bodies. It matters that our bodies express and embody an intention, an awareness. I would dare to say it matters that from time to time we *kneel*. Three of the words that most distress me in contemporary liturgical practice are 'kneel or sit'. Kneeling is fine, sitting is fine. But 'kneel or sit', in so far as it implies that it doesn't much matter *what* you do with your body at this point, seems rather less helpful. If you sit, know what you are doing! Sit mindfully; put your breath in your belly and listen to your heartbeat and sit up straight. And if you are going to kneel, kneel for goodness' sake. It's not impossible! God gave us two knees to balance on and it doesn't kill us, even us frail moderns, actually to use our knees once in a while and kneel upright. For the life of the Trinity to live in us, soul, heart and body, day by day, does involve our thinking about what we are doing with, and as, our bodies. The famous exchange between St François de Sales and one of his enthusiastic female penitents comes to mind. 'I'll begin to talk to you about prayer,' said St François, 'when you have learned to talk more slowly, walk more slowly, and eat more slowly. How exactly do you expect to be a home in history for the eternal life of the Word's adoration if your very physical life is tense, distracted and fragmented? You need to learn something of yourself to pray with the fullest freedom and the fullest effect.' That's not some precious crypto-yogic wisdom. It is, rather, common sense. And as soon as we've begun to reflect on how we inhabit our bodies thoughtfully and prayerfully, of course we begin to think about how we relate generally to our world; how our wider habits, our social habits, our political and economic habits, express or fail to express the embodiment I've been talking about. Mindful presence, awareness of the divine life making its home in us now in the body of Christ, is something that ought to open the door to all kinds of questions and reflections about the doing of God's justice in our world. And there is, once again, no great gulf between the life of prayer and the life of action. We need to know that effective, thoughtful, intelligent and transforming action arises most dependably from attention in prayer of the kind I've been outlining.

I hope you can see some of the connections here where mission is concerned. Mission is an invitation to live in a new world. It's not recruiting people for a manifesto or a programme. It is an invitation. Our Lord in his ministry on earth does not give out forms to complete that you hand to somebody at the door. Our Lord breaks bread. Our Lord takes the hands of those who come to him. Our Lord transfigures the world he is in by his welcome. That's where mission starts: in our awareness that we have been welcomed, and that our task is to invite others into a new world. Of course, it's costly, because transformation always is, but unless the invitation is there at the heart it will always come across more as a demand than a gift. In thinking about mission we have to remind ourselves again and again and again that it is gift, not demand, that we are speaking of. The demand comes, God knows, as soon as the gift is received. The Jesus who welcomes people so freely and indiscriminately is also the Jesus who says, 'pick up your cross'. Let's not imagine that we're talking here about some bland invitation to a world that is not really all that different. But just as prayer, serious prayer, seems to begin in looking in wonder, in the gaze of astonishment, so with mission. What is this new world where things are so different? What is this new world where depths we hadn't imagined are uncovered and made visible?

The idea that our sacramental practice ought to be missional is one that is quite difficult to work out in detail, and is often rendered in unhelpful ways. But the sense in which it is obviously true is, of course, the sense in which our sacramental practice declares, 'This is how it is, this is the new world.' All that we surround our sacramental practice with, especially in the Catholic tradition, all that we do to say, 'this is special, this is worth attending to', is a way of saying, 'the world here is different'. Not different in the sense that this is a sort of 'Indian reservation' for people who like that sort of thing, but different in the sense of opening up what we miss again and again in our habitual life. The specialness of sacramental worship, the splendour and the beauty of sacramental worship, are ways, under God's grace, of opening our eyes day by day, not of giving ourselves an occasional experience of intense enjoyment.

The mission implications of what I've been saying really have to do very simply with the assumption I started with: the Church is because God is and God acts. What God does, is, enacts in the Church, is that state of affairs in creation when creatures lovingly and delightedly know their origin and their goal, otherwise known as the kingdom of heaven. Mission needs to be about an invitation to the kingdom of heaven. To understand the Church in this light and to understand prayer in this light is our way into seeing mission afresh in relation to that kingdom; the kingdom that, as one of the great apocryphal sayings from the so-called Gospel of Thomas says, is 'spread abroad upon the earth but we do not see it'. That means that our mission and our prayer alike are not first and foremost enterprises we undertake in order to get a result. Mission is not the desperate attempt to sign up more people, prayer is not the desperate attempt to cross the infinite gulf between us and God. Both begin in the givenness of God's act, the manifesting and opening of the new world in Jesus. It's there, it's been done, 'it is finished'. This is how it is. And that's the mystery and the gift to which our mission must always return and to which our prayer must always bear witness. If we have a contribution to make in a muddled and anxious Church, it must be, surely, in this recognition, this grateful awareness of the 'already happening' character of the kingdom, the sense that we are and we act and we speak and we pray because God is and God acts.

2

The Gift of the Trinity in Mission

ALISON MILBANK

No book on mission would be complete without some consideration of God's own action towards the world he gave us. The word 'mission' in Scripture does not primarily describe our own activity but that of the Persons of the Trinity, especially in St John's Gospel, where the sendings of the Son and the Spirit are described. 'I have come down from heaven, not to do my own will, but the will of him who sent me' (John 6.38), says our Lord. To recognize Jesus as the one sent is to acknowledge he comes from the Father and is the beginning of a recognition of the trinitarian relations. 'The Church's mission', as Gilles Emery writes in his fine study, 'is an extension of this sending' (Emery, 2011, p. 26). The procession of the Holy Spirit is the vital agent of our sending and our recognition: 'God has sent the Spirit of his Son into our hearts, crying, "Abba! Father!"' (Gal. 4.6). It is by the temporal processions of the Son and the Spirit that we and the angels are brought into union with God and the whole creation returns to its maker.

It is for this reason that the Holy Trinity has been seen by Protestants and Catholics alike as missional and why this doctrine has returned to the centrality it deserves in Christian thought and practice. Lesslie Newbigin describes it 'not as an intellectual capstone which can be put on the top of the arch at the very end, on the contrary what Athanasius called it, the "arche" the presupposition without which the preaching of the Gospel in a pagan world cannot begin' (Newbigin, 1963, p. 36). With our faithful adherence to credal faith,

Anglo-Catholicism has always embraced this doctrine joyfully. I recall as a child hearing the traditional Anglican Missal last Gospel reading with the wonderful cadences of the Prologue to St John's Gospel, and the excitement of our common genuflection at the world-shattering moment of 'and the Word was made flesh'. I felt in my own sudden descent to the ground the awful humility and realism of God's humility and solidarity with us in the dust of physicality.

I want therefore in this chapter to look at our tradition and charism and discern ways in which we can today draw out treasures old and new through the Trinity to enrich our evangelism and give us new confidence in holding to the value of our worship, not as a fusty inheritance but as a living flame, warm enough to melt atheist hearts and clear enough to satisfy contemporary longings for truth. This doctrine is not a set of words so much as a gift: God communicates himself to us as holiness, as becoming incarnate, and as relationality itself.

Sometimes in recent attention to the social Trinity as a blueprint for human and ecclesial organization, the Trinity has been treated as a chemical formula, an abstraction or template. So too in some usages of the Trinity in mission, where we are told that the mission is God's – true enough – but that we are a bit extraneous. We can join in, if we can catch up, but are somehow separate. There is the model in God like a template, and a separate group of humans to whom that template acts as a guide. That is where the heart of Catholic mission in prayer, about which Rowan Williams wrote in Chapter 1, is a corrective. For the Catholic – indeed, for classic Anglican writers such as Richard Hooker – the Church is a supernatural society (Hooker, 1841, pp. xv, 1, 2, 217) and has its life and its being in God. It was to assert the holiness of the Church that John Keble got up to give his Assize sermon that inaugurated the Oxford Movement. In God, as Paul said, 'we live and move and have our being' (Acts 17.28). Our life is communal, 'God knows us in his Church' (de Lubac, 1956, p. 45), for that is the life of the Trinity. As Henri de Lubac writes: 'even more than an institution, [the Church] is a life that is passed on' (de Lubac, 1956, p. 36). By baptism we are impelled by the Spirit into relation with Christ and brought to call God, Father. That is how we live here, now and every minute, in this trinitarian life by participation. The anathema of the Athanasian creed is right in an existential sense, in that without this indwelling we simply perish. To live in the Spirit is to live in this relationality of charity and of gift. It is important that when the language of gift-giving is used to describe mission, we realize that what is given is this mode of life, which has a particular character. It is to that habitus or form I now turn to discern distinctive marks of trinitarian mission, and suggest some practical outworking of that mode of life in communicating it to others.

Our first mark is holiness. One of the paradoxes of the development of the doctrine of the Trinity in the early Church was that it was led by a sense that the reality of God is a mystery beyond our capacity to understand it. What theologians call the economic Trinity – how we are saved, how we have experienced the divine – led to an ever greater sense of God's otherness and what is often called the immanent Trinity. Defining trinitarian relations therefore was the opposite of trying to put God in a box; rather, it was a way to pray truthfully. Christians sing the Sanctus, 'Holy, holy, holy, Lord God of hosts', imitating the heavenly beings, to acknowledge this otherness. We recall that it was the sinful and inadequate Isaiah who heard these words, flung from seraph to seraph across the temple as they flew, and it was out of this powerful awareness of the awefulness of God's mysterious life that his mission began and he could say: 'Here am I; send me!' (Isa. 6.8).

And that is where, I believe, Catholic mission always begins, in our particularly strong witness to the holiness and otherness of God's transcendence. Homely or festal, our worship proclaims this by the special clothes, the silence, the dignity of the words, the formal gestures, the reverence. We can misuse all this by turning reverence to formalism and making a solemn Mass into a performance rather than an act of worship, but at its most sincere our worship bears witness to God's holiness and the call to become holy. It may just be the increasing old age and incapacity of congregations, but most Christians have given up kneeling. Anglo-Catholics, by contrast, still kneel – as Christ knelt when he prayed. We bow to acknowledge the Trinity in the 'Glory be'; we maintain canon 18 of the 1604 Canons of the Church of England by reverencing the name of Jesus in worship.

We make these gestures because, like Lewis's Aslan, our God is holy and even dangerous, but all the more attractive and compelling for that otherness. 'In the juvescence of the year, came Christ the tiger', wrote T. S. Eliot in *Gerontion* (Eliot, 1974, p. 39). Our God has the vivid energy and potential power we see in the great cats. The most informal liturgy can respect this quality of the divine as much as the most elevated, when every action is done with meaning and reverence.

Our missional impetus in worship should then be to engender this sense of God's holiness and our own as made in his image. The point about the transcendence of God is that we discern this, as Augustine of Hippo did long ago, by looking inside and seeing our own mysterious depths. Offering well-being events that are so managed as to draw people beyond self-curation into a deeper engagement with reality through Christian spiritual practices is the obvious place to start to engender a sense of the divine and our own holiness. I would suggest, however, that the sacrament of baptism is another opportunity to draw people more deeply into God's transcendence. There is a temptation to turn the baptism of a child from a family who do not regularly worship into a party. While the festive is one core element, it can leave the family spiritually where they began. It can be more transformative and more missional to stress the theological significance of a rescue from the powers of evil. Every parent knows full well the evil forces that surround their beloved child in a violent and greedy world, so the symbolic and real power of being claimed by Christ as his own, sealed with holy oil, is something to emphasize. In baptism the child is made holy and becomes a way to open a sense of the transcendence among her or his parents, as they recognize the depths of meaning and divine orientation in the infant. We need only a few words to draw this out, and real reverence. The aim is to stir up a desire for a beyond, a longing for meaning and purpose, which the child already represents in the life of a couple. It is the beginning of that trinitarian movement from Galatians 4.6: 'God has sent the Spirit of his Son into our hearts, crying, "Abba! Father!"' The party afterwards will be all the more joyful for a sense of rescue, and of the mystery that the child represents.

Our world is crying out for this otherness at every level. Our public and social ethics, for example, lack a strong orientation to the common good because it cannot work unless people acknowledge a beyond to call them to account and ground their communality. As knowledge of history dies, so does any sense that the world could be different from the way it is now. And yet there remains, as Henri de Lubac taught, a natural desire for God in the human person. And so, hearts are still restless, but have nowhere to aim their desire. 'Our heart is restless unless it rests in you' (Augustine, 1991, p. 3). It is interesting to see how Goth culture still clings to the interstices of the sacred with its use of religious symbols. Even when inverted they act as a negative provocation of meaning in holy objects that seem to promise some sense of significance. Similarly, in a Church Army research project (Hollinghurst, 2010, pp. 191–2) unchurched young people were asked what worship might attract them. Surprisingly, it was not soft rock and screens but candles and incense that they cited. We see the same tendency in television drama, where a priest is always conveniently lurking among his church's crepuscular Gothic columns, and the candles are lit, even though no service is going on. In both cases, there is an attempt to symbolize transcendence, even though many people will deny they believe in God. Secularism in our country is a loss of habits of worship, of sacred time, of anchorage in morality and holiness. So we should be on the alert for the impulse of desire for God breaking out in odd places such as reverence akin to worship of the dead, in the belief in an afterlife – among those who claim no belief in God – and in the very prevalent belief in angels. All these popular focuses of the holy have a place in our theology and worship, where we can direct them to a deeper faith.

While, therefore, it is important to be missional in making our worship hospitable and open, we should not seek to dumb it down in the service of comprehension, for what we are calling people to is a mystery, not a set of mathematical formulae. A former colleague of mine was converted to Christianity by watching the Community of the Resurrection at prayer. At first, he did not understand what they were doing, but their activity was wholly significant and captivating in its strangeness. In Christian mission we offer a person, Jesus, but one who is both wholly ours and yet wholly beyond our capacity to understand him. And what we call people to realize is that this is also true of anyone: the more we know and love someone, the deeper we come to know their inner, hidden being. It is that sense of a relationship as an ever deepening discovery that keeps it alive.

We also need to stress the transcendence of God when debating with New Age believers. There is much in our worship that attracts such people, who honour the natural world, and seek to make rituals that embody the seasons. We too acknowledge the holiness of nature as we bless holy wells, honour shrines, and use the body and its senses in worship. To worship pure nature, however, is to baptize violence, to be close to an idea also that one can manipulate the divine in a quasi-magical way. The trinitarian stress on God's mystery, and being the cause of nature, prevents this. It tells us that we cannot manipulate God. God is the creator of all that is through the Son, who shapes and makes it intelligible, and the Spirit who undergirds and pervades it. God as Creator is not an old man on a cloud, but the Trinity in unity of action. When some people say they do not believe in God they have this William Paley picture of a divine watchmaker with a beard, who winds up the cosmos and withdraws, whereas a true transcendence sees God holding the world in being at every instant. As generations of missionaries to non-Christian parts of the world have found, the Trinity comes early in proclamation, not at the end – the arche not the capstone in Newbigin's words quoted above – and is a really important corrective to false conceptions of God. To speak of God as a oneness of relations of self-giving love is very helpful to New Age or pagan believers; to speak of the equality within the godhead, in which the Persons are co-eternal and co-equal, speaks to a society very concerned with equality in principle, if wedded to inequality in practice. God has no gender, but revelation has taught us to call him Father. There is a case, I believe, for continuing the ancient Syrian practice of thinking of the Spirit in maternal terms as a way of signalling the truth of baptism, that femininity as well as masculinity comes from God and is capable of divinization. Our reverence for the Blessed Virgin is important here also. Yet if New Age pagan pantheism needs transcendence, Anglo-Catholicism needs a fresh appreciation of the holiness of the natural world, which is not just acknowledged at the level of ecotheology, but also plays out in our liturgical life.

A second mark of trinitarian life is embodiment; by the incarnation, the child in the manger is God himself, so that to see Christ is to see the Father. If the atonement has been the defining doctrine of traditional evangelicalism, ours has been the taking of flesh into the godhead. This was due to the return to patristic sources by the Tractarians and by the strong influence of F. D. Maurice on the second generation of the Oxford Movement. The *Lux Mundi* essay collection of 1889, edited by Gore – which sought to ally this doctrine with scientific thought – put the crown on incarnationalism. The doctrine lay behind the radical politics and Christian Socialism of so many of our forebears, from Charles Marston and Conrad Noel to Ken Leech. It is clear in the report *A Time to Sow* by the Centre for Theology and Community (Thorlby,

2017), on Anglo-Catholic church growth in London, that this incarnational community engagement continues to be a key factor in successful outreach, though now it tends to be shown in involvement in what is going on locally, rather than purely ecclesial initiatives. It is something the evangelical model of church planting has learnt from us, so that where once some evangelical parishes were uneasy about social work as taking one away from the core evangelistic activity, now it is the first thing they look to do. Moreover, incarnational language is used by official church reports, such that one is encouraged to be incarnate, as it were, in a particular place.

That language of incarnation to describe what Christians do is a little troubling, since we are not God. We are physical beings, and wherever we live and work is given to us. We do not take humanity upon us as the Son does, and we need to be careful how we understand our embodiment. And yet we can say that the Church is a continuation of the incarnation as we share the missions of the Son and the Spirit, by a sense of being sent as love and wisdom, God's gifts to his world, carrying on the temporal missions of what are sometimes called the Father's two hands. Whether the pews or chairs are full or empty, if a church is deeply engaged in the lives and communities of the parish, its ministry has this incarnational character, and its priestly intercession connects and returns that society to God. For intercession is true mission, in which we come close to the needs, desires and struggles of our situation and offer them to God in the Spirit and through Christ. It has a trinitarian grammar and is a good way to help lay people to understand how we live in the Trinity as we discern the Spirit at work in our world, and obediently pray through Christ, returning all to the Father. To know you are prayed for is powerful missionally. It is easy to text or send cards through letterboxes to let people know. Church websites can offer places to ask for prayer. But we must never neglect our own needs as a Church. I have known a parish pray for everyone in need, but not mention their own desperate need for money. Certainly, prayer is not magic, but it is a mystery in which anything is possible as we seek to align our wills with the Divine.

Mission with the incarnation at its heart is necessarily sacramental, by which participation in the divine is effected. Here worship again is the beginning of our mission because of its Eucharistic basis. Worship that is reverent and takes God seriously is confident because it trusts in the reality of what it is doing, that in worship we join Christ's own offering at the heavenly altar. The Church is undergoing a great crisis of confidence because of attacks upon us, on our history and on faith generally. Even in a tiny cathedral town such as my own, my appearance in the street in a cassock can provoke real animosity. It is easy to retreat to the private, to avoid the streets, to apologize. And although, like all institutions, there are many things of which the Church should repent, not least the abuse of children and young people, that is different from an apologetic attitude to our faith in Jesus Christ. Yet secularism is as strong within the Church as without: it runs through us all. And it is here that trinitarian doctrine again comes to our aid. For, according to classic Christian doctrine, God is a wholly positive, free outpouring of life and love, without passion, without lack. It was through the living out of this fullness and self-giving that Christ was able to offer humanity back to God, in spite of – and indeed through – his passionate, tempted human nature. To be part of the missions of the Son and the Spirit is to share in this wholly positive character of gift. Eucharistic worship takes physical stuff, the bread and wine of a human world of injustice, scarcity and effort, and returns them to us as fullness of being and charity. There is always enough, as the miracles of the loaves and fishes and the wedding at Cana tell us. For, as Angel Mendez Montoya reminds us in his *Theology of Food*, 'the Eucharistic feasting is participation in and performance of (within a complex dimension of space and time) divine caritas' (Mendez Montoya, 2009, p. 156) that is the infinite life of God himself. Mission in Roman Catholic theology also proceeds in this manner as adumbrated by Bevans and Schroeder: 'the church's mission-ary nature derives from its participation in this overflowing trinitarian life' (Bevans and Schroeder, 2004, p. 289).

As the Orthodox have taught us, in worship we humans enter an eternal realm: we leave time. In our gestures and pace, our music and words, we model the life of heaven. In this realm all is possible: total forgiveness and reconciliation; complete transformation of us and the world. We live suspended from Paradise like a child in the cradle. 'Our weight', as Augustine taught us, 'is our love' (Augustine, 1991, p. 278). This is the remaking of reality and it is missional, if done out of that overflowing charity. That is the key, that in the priestly and diaconal actions within the rite – and with the whole people of God who are involved and make this priestly action – the Church offers itself and the world to God. When we so act, the liturgy can speak by its performative character. Because some-thing happens to the elements and to us: we are taken up in the whole trinitarian and incarnational action.

I would like to see the Eucharist celebrated in marketplaces, in parks, in homes. Let us have confidence in its power and do all we can to help it speak to our congregations as well as those beyond. For the former, it could be a Mass in slow motion, or sections taken week by week and gently and briefly expounded; for the latter, as we know from baptisms, just a word or two to shape and open the action can do a great deal. The attempt to separate the *Missio Dei* from liturgy makes no sense from the perspective of the doctrine of participation. Robert Chapman, in his doctorate on Eucharist and mission, points out how throughout Anglican theology, from the Reformation to today, deification and participation in God have been central to our Eucharistic thought (Chapman, 2015). This logic under-girds the extra-liturgical blessings of homes or people before key moments in their lives; or the development, which is so welcome, of passion plays and other dramatic enactments of the Christian story – like the diocese of St Albans's wonderful puppets and the radical Red Cross St George's poetic liturgy.

Mission begins and ends with the Eucharist, but out of it flows activities that embody that trinitarian movement of procession and return. The gospel procession itself enacts the mission of God and the whole narrative of the incarnation.

The Eucharist is the overflowing heart of the extra-liturgical, by which this transformation of the material is effected. We bless new homes, people, objects, by which they are recognized as God's own making and restored to their origin in God, as Andrew Davison's book *Blessing* (Davison, 2014, p. 3) reminds us. Here again our incarnational witness can become missional. We should publicly offer blessing before university, a new job, moving home, or going into hospital, or after recovery from illness. I would love to see a new churching of women, in which the risk and danger of childbirth is allied to Christ's passion, and offered to anyone. Many people will be comfortable calling us in, rather like calling in the plumber – more than we ever realize.

The sacrament of penance, which similarly takes its being from the rites of baptism and Eucharist, is another way in which we can offer that transformative reconnection with God. I recall a teenage boy rushing into the cathedral one evening in late December. He was somewhat incoherent, but it quickly emerged that he wanted to confess a bad relationship. I do not think he had ever been in a church before, but he knelt down and made a simple confession, and we got him safely on the bus back to Nottingham. The point about these rites for the individual is that they can reach into every aspect of people's lives, from divorce to bereavement. Rather than special rites for the faithful, we should see them as outward-facing, incarnational ministry, in which the work of the Spirit is acknowledged, and through Christ the people concerned are reconnected with their heavenly Father.

A third mark of the life of the Trinity is its relational character. The Eucharist, by its very nature, is a communal rite, and as trinitarian worshippers we honour what Ken Leech called 'The Social God'. This communality has been used by some to justify very wide differences in what the nature of a local church might be, under the rubric of diversity. Yet diversity in the sense of Trinitarian Persons is only a way of expressing the difference of relations within the Godhead. The Father is Father in relation to the Son, the Spirit is the Spirit of the Father given to the Son, so that in the West we may speak of 'proceeding from the Father and the Son'. From Augustine onwards, we have spoken of the Spirit as the love between the Father and the Son. The Trinity is unified and acts as one through different modes of action. The celebrated mixed economy of churches can only be justified through the Trinity if the different congregations in an area are related in some way. By all means have a Messy Church, which is quite similar to the traditional afternoon Sunday school model or the old midweek craft club. Yet such a group would flourish better if allowed to be porous to the whole local church community, not a separate end in itself for all time. For example, the group could make artwork or prepare drama to share at a Sunday Eucharist. We are called, in the trinitarian life, to be related: to live in communion. All our missional outworkings should have some way to enable people to move further on and further in.

For what we have to offer our fragmented world is just that: a faith in the understanding of the human as a social being, who finds himself or herself in the communion of life in God, which is the Church. Welfare officers in universities inform us that life for many students today, which one might imagine as highly communal, is in reality very lonely, and that even clubbing has waned and public sociability of all sorts. Student societies, like all political and social organizations, are shrinking in size. Social media could, in theory, really aid real bodily meeting and networking, but this is less and less the case. This goes along with a huge increase in anxiety among young people, which increases in universities exponentially year by year, and the appalling figures of self-harm among young people. I am building meditation exercises into every class for my first-year students. It was significant that in the *Time to Sow* report, young people's choirs were a constant feature among the growing parishes. This may appear to be a supremely old-fashioned mode of connection, and yet communal singing is powerful in terms of emotional release, providing a sense of belonging and an opening to the beyond, as early French socialists such as Charles Fourier, among others, found. At St George in the East, the midweek choir club sings at Sunday Mass once a month. In St Wulfram's Grantham, the church music director takes a singing lesson weekly in several primary schools, so that it is not unusual to find over 30 children singing on a Sunday morning, with of course their parents in attendance. St John's Catford has a choristers' club. Music, in which the voices blend and each part exists in relation to the other, has long been a theological expression of community, of concord.

When Dante in his *Divine Comedy* reaches the Empyrean, he has a vision of the Church triumphant as a glorious creamy rose, with souls forming petals and the angels as the bees, pollinating them with praise and insight. Then his final vision is the Trinity itself, as three circles, two rainbow-hued and one breathing fire. Within the circles he discerns the human form, and he tries, beyond his capacity, to understand how this humanity of Christ relates to the divine, when his vision fails, and yet, 'my desire and will were turned, like a wheel revolving evenly/ by the love that moves the sun and the other stars' (Dante, *Paradiso* 33.143–5). His own flesh and desire become the site of a knowledge his mind cannot fathom. All Christians proclaim the goodness and beauty of the physical and the bodily, but Catholics have it as their particular charism. It is the only justification for the embrace of art, music and all the senses in the beauty of holiness. 'I will not cease from honouring matter because it was through matter that my salvation came to pass', as John of Damascus wrote (Allies, 1898, p. 16). We live in a very abstract culture, in which our language is becoming less vivid and material and in which the ability to edit images of ourselves alienates us from our own bodies, as I see again in students whose identification photograph for their records often bears little relation to the person in the flesh. The body becomes an object to lavish care and money upon in order to try to produce an unreal perfection.

Christians have been afraid to challenge all this for fear of seeming judgemental in a climate that already thinks them puritanical. What we can offer, however, is a human solidarity in which the messy physicality of our bodies is itself valued, and the body restored to reverence. This must not be divorced from the claims of the environment and ecological thinking, but thought of holistically and be in accord with Catholic support for the unborn child, the old and the disabled. We have not been Catholic enough in our ethical thinking, or imaginative enough in its expression in practice or liturgy. We have a great tradition of care for the poor and the outcast, and of theological orthodoxy expressed in political radicalism. We have Anglican Catholic priest scholars like John Rodwell and Michael North-cott working in the field of environmental ethics, but where is this work in our mission? The interdependence of the social, the physical and the holy should lead us towards the kind of evangelistic proclamation that Pope Francis offers in *Laudato Si'*, with its powerful denunciation of how we have despoiled 'our sister, Mother Earth' and 'forgotten that we ourselves are dust of the earth (cf. Gen. 2.7); our very bodies are made up of her elements, we breathe her air and we receive life and refreshment from her waters' (Francis I, 2015, p. 2). Too often we separate what is thought of as social concern from evangelism, and yet what is more compelling than Pope Francis's presentation of nature as created? 'Nature is usually seen as a system which can be studied, understood and controlled, whereas creation can only be understood as a gift from the out-stretched hand of the Father of all, and as a reality illuminated by the love which calls us together into universal communion' (Francis I, 2015, p. 76). Again, we can hear that note of the transcendent as grounding our wonder and our sociality. For this encyclical offers an integral ecology in which the needs of the poor and of the earth go together.

Our salvation, then, comes from an awareness of the holiness of matter and its assumption by God himself. Our mission to call people to sociality is part of a call to reverence physicality and our own bodies, as well as the natural world, to see the earth as a great grail. Following the New Testament practice from Pentecost onwards, we have always grounded our evangelism in Christ, but in the world of today we have to start further back, by making people aware of the idea of God and of a deeper reality than that which we see, credible and attractive, and the creaturely humanity and way of being that flows from this. We do not necessarily need a raft of philosophical arguments, but we do need a sense of what the world, experience and relationships look like from this perspective – the whole *habitus* or ecology of Christian life. In Charles Dickens's great novel *Bleak House* the dying child crossing-sweeper has no idea of God at all, until the doctor teaches him the 'Our Father' and he learns what the love of a physical father, which he has never known, might be like through knowledge of a divine parent. Establishing the divine is just a beginning, because the way of Christ has to be followed back from alienation and rebellion to obedience and self-giving, but a beginning it is, and Christ as Son and Word in the context of a Trinity is one helpful place to begin.

I have outlined some key features of Catholic mission in the Trinity: holiness, incarnational embrace of physicality, relationality, and showed their interconnection. I have emphasized the impassibility of God, that mission should share the serene and positive welling-up of never-failing streams, even and especially when your congregation consists of three old ladies and a dog. Henri de Lubac, in *The Splendour of the Church*, reminds us that the Church is always 'a ship full of unruly passengers who seem to be on the point of wrecking it' (de Lubac, 1956, p. 113). Yet we lack confidence, all of us. We are weakened by our divisions from being the force in the Church of England we once were. We are less connected to our theological resources, which, paradoxically, are in the intellectual ascendant. We cannot just celebrate a lovely Mass and believe that will save the world. It will, of course, but its serene outflow must penetrate every aspect of our public and communal life. Christ is King: this is his world, which he made, entered and died for, and he will offer it back to the Father. Only a mission that is truly trinitarian in offering a whole way of life, with truth that embraces every aspect of existence, will work. We must be bolder, to challenge the demonic powers of greed and injustice, of lust and cruelty. We must bring Christ into every cultural, social and political debate, because we believe in a God who is truth. The Trinity is a way of life. Paradoxically, it is because faith calls us out of 'the world' understood as a self-subsisting whole, entire to itself, that we can transform it sacramentally. Only Catholic mission, in the end, can truly 'baptize culture', because of our transcendent grounding in the otherness of God.

Perhaps the most characteristic quality that Anglo-Catholics derive from our root in the Trinity is beauty, and not just meaning aesthetic perfection, although that is important. Holiness is beautiful, when seen in the serenity of the elderly religious, in the joyfulness of the gospel choir, in the whole action of worship. There is a beauty about the Catholic way of life, its saints and customs that gives you a sense of homesickness for heaven, longing, in the words of W. H. Auden, 'that we, too, may come to the picnic / With nothing to hide, join the dance / As it moves in perichoresis / Turns about the abiding tree' (Auden, 1991, p. 641). We can be cliquey, clericalist, bitchy, but at our best we offer pure beauty, which is nourished by truth, that really lives and breathes a divine air. Dostoevsky's idiot, Prince Myshkin, was reported as saying that beauty will save the world. His descent into madness and silence might make us question those words, but perhaps not. For it is Christ's foolish beauty that redeems us. He makes himself ugly by embracing the way that leads to a cross but offers in this way an inclusive beauty that makes everything and everyone lovely. 'He hung deformed upon the cross, but his deformity was our beauty', says Augustine (Jeffrey, 2017, p. 45). This is our charism: to see in everyone and everything the potentially beautiful and to make worship and holy places that catch the breath and awaken that longing for God in his loveliness and infinite love. As David Bentley Hart observes: 'the true infinite lies outside and all about this enclosed universe of strife and shadows; it shows itself as beauty and as light: not totality, nor again chaos, but the music of a triune God' (Hart, 2003, p. 315).

Bibliography

Allies, M. (1898), *John of Damascus on Holy Images*, London: Thomas Baker.

Auden, W. H. (1991), *Collected Poems*, Edward Mendelson (ed.), New York: Vintage.

Augustine of Hippo (1991), *Confessions*, trans. Henry Chadwick, Oxford: Oxford University Press.

Bevans, Stephen B. and Roger P. Schroeder (2004), *Constants in Context: A Theology of Mission for Today*, New York: Orbis.

Chapman, Robert (2015), 'Eucharistic Sacrifice as Missionary Gift in Mission-shaped Church', PhD dissertation, Archbishop's Examination in Theology.

Davison, Andrew (2014), *Blessing*, London: SCM Press.

De Lubac, Henri (1956), *The Splendour of the Church*, trans. Michael Mason, London: Sheed and Ward.

Eliot, T. S. (1974), *Collected Poems 1909–1962*, London: Faber.

Emery, Gilles (2011), *The Trinity: An Introduction to Catholic Doctrine on the Triune God*, trans. Matthew Levering, Washington, DC: Catholic University of America.

Francis I (2015), *Laudato Si'*, online at www.vatican.va/content/ francesco/en/encyclicals/documents/papa-francesco_20150524_enciclica-laudato-si.html.

Hart, David (2003), *The Beauty of the Infinite: The Aesthetics of Christian Truth*, Grand Rapids, MI: Eerdmans.

Hollinghurst, Steve (2010), *Mission-shaped Evangelism: The Gospel in Contemporary Culture*, Norwich: Canterbury Press.

Hooker, Richard (1841), *Works of Richard Hooker*, 2 vols, Isaac Walton (ed.), Oxford: Oxford University Press.

Jeffrey, David Lyle (2017), *The Beauty of Holiness: Art and the Bible in Western Culture*, Grand Rapids, MI: Eerdmans.

Mendez Montoya, Angel F. (2009), *The Theology of Food: Eating and the Eucharist*, Oxford: Wiley-Blackwell.

Newbigin, Lesslie (1963), *Trinitarian Doctrine for Today's Mission*, Edinburgh: Edinburgh House Press.

Thorlby, Tim (2017), *A Time to Sow: Anglican Catholic Church Growth in London*, The Centre for Theology and Community.

3

Catholic Mission – God's Mission as Our Mission

LUKE MILLER

There was once a churchwarden who would sit near the door of the church. A few minutes into the service she would quietly get up, lock the door, and return to her place. The new vicar asked her why she did this, and she replied: 'We must lock the door, Father, or someone might come in.'

Do you want your church to grow? To be honest, we are a bit screwed up about this. We are uncomfortable with concern about numbers in church and what can seem to be trying to measure success as though we were some business. What are we measuring? Even if all our churches had 1,000 communicants each week we would only be scratching the surface of the need. Is it not really the case that all churches are equally unsuccessful?

There is a view, which a priest of the older generation once put very forcefully to me, that God is at work in the world, and the Holy Spirit will call people to church. When they come, our job is to pastor them, and the parishes that run best in this way become great centres of pastoral care and support. That in itself could be missional, for people were attracted to the community that was formed and delighted to be part of it. This pastoral model is not, however, good enough. By and large it results in institutional decline, but that is not the point. It abandons Catholic life. Unless we are actively evangelizing we are not living as Catholic Christians.

In what follows the case will be made that as Catholic Anglicans we should want to grow, and practical suggestions will be offered for action that will result in numerical growth. It will be shown that not only is mission an integral part of Catholic Christianity, but the actions we take to evangelize are simply Catholic practice. In a more practical section some consideration will then be given to the current context of mission for Catholic Anglicans in contemporary Britain, and finally there will be a section on the tenets and methods of Catholic mission.

In much of this, reference will be made to the writing of Father George Congreve (see Woodgate, 1956, and James, 2019; my own book on the Cowley Fathers is forthcoming). Congreve was one of the early Cowley Fathers (see James, 2019), whose writings, though largely forgotten, are a significant contribution to many aspects of Anglican Catholic life, including missiology.

Mission is a Catholic gift and integral to being a Catholic Christian

Congreve said that church growth begins with personal growth, for the one soul that anyone can really help to convert is one's own. For Congreve, therefore, the root of all mission is personal holiness. Speaking to newly professed sisters he said, 'Dedication is itself a "result already attained" such that the question of success or outcome passes away.' This is not something whose success can be measured. We must reject 'the amateur industry of works to relieve the burden of idleness', but the love of God breaks out in activity for the gospel such that 'there cannot be a living member of Christ in idleness' (Congreve, 1874–1914, Book 1).

This is mission founded on personal self-sacrifice and personal holiness. It is not initiated by the missioner, but is a response to Christ who reached out to us first in the mission of the incarnation; it is an imitation of Christ's dedication to the Father, who on entering the world said, 'I have come to do your will'

(Heb. 10.7). This was the vision statement for the incarnation, and its mission action plan.

Congreve wrote that the result of obedient self-giving to God is a missionary desire to share this first love with others. Self-offering leads out into mission:

> It is participation in the Divine Nature that makes every consideration necessarily secondary to the soul's personal relation to God. But this is the opposite of selfishness and is the only thing that actually turns us away from selfishness. (Congreve, 1890–1917, p. 98)

Mission is therefore not simply obedience to the Great Commission to 'go therefore and make disciples of all nations, baptizing them in the name of the Father and of the Son and of the Holy Spirit' (Matt. 28.19), but a response to the fact that 'Christ has taken human nature and made all one'. To help in the salvation of souls is therefore not 'accidental, but vital for every Christian'. This might be 'parents at home, or *missionaries* abroad' (Congreve, 1913).

This means that the things that help the growth of the congregation in *depth* help the growth of the Church in *number*: being busy about the sacraments; personal prayer; confession; catechesis; habits of holiness; the consecration of home life by simple things like helping our people to say grace at meals, or pray with their children. The new Alexa Church of England skill allows users to ask for grace to be said at meals. This and similar ways to offer routes to prayer and personal holiness should not be seen as gimmicks, but as part of this basic work of equipping souls to grow in faith and love.

Can we measure this?

It would be a mistake to say that since mission begins internally and spiritually it cannot be measured, and that parish annual returns are useless and any fixation with numbers is wrong.

Spiritual growth in depth that cannot be measured leads to forms of growth that it *is* possible to quantify.

Gallup, the pollster, is supposed to have said that if you don't measure what you value you come to value what you measure. There is a point therefore in the anxious vicar looking at the services register and asking, 'Were we more than last week; more than this time last year?' There are meaningful measurements that can be made. While 'repent, believe the gospel' is not measurable, it is possible to measure response to the second half of Jesus' saying: 'and follow me'. The assent might not be measurable but the action that is the symptom of the assent is measurable, a thing and not an idea.

Measurement is not merely recording of mission; it achieves mission. A chaplaincy in an institution will have measurable results in terms of fewer days off, fewer drop-outs, even fewer suicides; this measurable data can justify the mission and make a compelling case for funding it, for by monetizing the value of the outcomes the case can be made to the institution that it is cheaper for them to have a chaplain than not to do so. Counting what is measurable enables activity that has immeasurable effects on souls.

A local church is therefore well advised to measure its work in the community, which can lead to benefits such as grants or publication on public websites of church activities. Fundamental to all we do is the community of prayer and worship. By the very fact that it meets the congregation is combating loneliness and social isolation. Church music is a contribution to the cultural life of the community – maybe. There are studies showing the economic and social benefits of a parish church (see, for example, Sunde, 2016, quoting Wood-Daly, 2016). This may feel like uncomfortable language, but it is language that helps the Church get a voice in the public square, a voice that can be used for the proclamation of the gospel.

Measuring activity helps to direct it and to determine what is simply displacement activity and what is actually helping. What do all those hours producing the community magazine or at meetings in the school produce? For many, the experience is that visiting the congregation in their homes is massively helpful in making sure newcomers persist in attendance and supporting the discipleship and commitment of longstanding members. Measuring impact can help to show whether pastors are over-visiting a small number of people or failing to use their time well, falling into the temptation to engage in cosy chats with congenial people rather than visiting as ministers of the gospel.

Beyond catechesis and prayer with people, studies from syna-gogues show that if you visit the home before the wedding or the funeral, or as soon as someone begins to come to worship, it is possible to invite the newcomer to collaborate in the vision for the development of the congregation, rather than being frustrated by perceived shortcomings or strangeness. Such a visit means the newcomer is twice as likely to stay in the con-gregation. The visitor might say, for example, that the music is shocking; and the pastor could respond: 'I am working on that and you can support me.' This collaborative approach is emphatically not the same as landing new people with a job as they come through the door.

The SIAMS (Statutory Inspection of Anglican and Methodist Schools) schedule (Church of England, 2005, 2019) offers some ways to assess what might be thought to be immeasurable. Strand 3 on the character and moral development of pupils states that in a Good Church school:

> There is a demonstrable culture of aspiring to be the best you can be: the person God created you to be. Pupils say how the school's Christian vision and associated values help them to make positive choices about how they live and behave. Pupils say how the school's Christian vision and associated values supports them in their learning.

It can be salutary to ask whether our church would be a Good Church school on this basis.

There are further challenges in Strand 6 on collective worship, and it is well worth reflecting on how this description, suitably adapted for the church setting, invites modification of some approaches in the local church:

> In a Good Church school ... Worship is invitational, offering everyone the opportunity to engage whilst allowing the freedom for those of other faiths and none to be present with integrity. All those who wish to be so are actively engaged in worship. Prayer is a natural and valued part of the culture of the school. It is not compulsory or forced. All those who wish to do so will have regular opportunities to pray and reflect. Pupils talk about the value of prayer and reflection both in formal and informal contexts and how being still and reflective in their own lives can be helpful. As appropriate to context, pupils speak of their personal use of prayer and reflection. Pupils recognise that worship provides meaningful opportunities to contribute to their spiritual development.

It is not simply that churches can ask corporately how they would rate themselves against this, but clergy and lay leaders also can be challenged. In which of our congregations is it the normative case that 'As appropriate to context, [members of the congregation] speak of their personal use of prayer and reflection'? The schedule contains practical suggestions as to how to achieve these outcomes, which churches would be well advised to read and consider using.

Counting can help and measuring and evaluating is useful to target activity, and improve outcomes from it. There is, however, a caution. Congreve helpfully taught that mission is necessary not for numbers, but for personal holiness:

> When a church loses its missionary enthusiasm and allows indifference as to the conversion of heathen nations, their own Christianity begins to die out, as it happens to the British Church refusing to join in the conversion of the hated Saxons. (Congreve, 1904)

To bring the good news, he continued, is not 'a favour that we do for the heathen, but a necessary instinctive action in our new nature of Christ in us'. Mission is both a symptom and a cause of growth in holiness. Mission, therefore, whatever its result in terms of numbers, is good for the Church. Understanding the beneficial results of mission influences how we evangelize.

Picking up on Ephesians 2.15, Congreve expanded on the benefit of being an evangelist. Because Christ is breaking down the barriers and making all one, there is already a link between those who evangelize and those who receive the message, and so, 'in turn we ourselves receive help and grace from those who are won to him'. The Church 'without them is incomplete, and all the members share in the enrichment of life in virtue which the conversion of each new member brings' (Congreve, 1904).

Mission is thus understood not to be a matter of sharing information for assent, but of inviting participation in a way of life, and so at its most basic evangelism is sharing Christian life and helping others to do the same. This need not be complicated. Enthusiasm for God can bubble out of us. People know things about one another and participate in small ways in the lives of colleagues – for example, knowing how someone likes their coffee; which, if any, football team they support; something perhaps of their tastes in music; their enthusiasms. The Christian can and should be as explicit about God and his Church and find ways to help others be similarly explicit.

This evangelism of enthusiasm must be properly directed. Is the missioner enthusiastic for Jesus, or for the institution or the liturgy or the music or the rite or the building? There is even a narcissistic evangelism in which Christ is obscured by the Christian. Congreve taught that self-sacrifice indeed connotes sacrifice.[1] While the evangelist's God-given personality is rightly, indeed necessarily, used in the work of the kingdom, it is not all about me, or our church, that jolly social club with hymns; these things must be sacrificed, for it is about Christ.

In *The Great Divorce*, C. S. Lewis has the image of the painter and paint: the artist who stops striving to learn and express more about the light he paints, but develops interest in the picture he paints and in the process of painting:

> Every poet and musician and artist, but for Grace, is drawn away from the love of the thing he tells, to love of the telling till, down in Deep Hell, they cannot be interested in God at all but only in what they say about Him. For it doesn't stop at being interested in paint, you know. They sink lower – becoming interested in their own personalities and then in nothing but their own reputations. (Lewis, 1945, p. 74)

Sacrifice, mortification, fasting, penitence, confession – all have their place in helping the missioner to let go of the things that humanity tends to put between ourselves and God: the institution, the rite, the vestments, the attractive externals that too often are taken seriously and not treated as adiaphora. The Christian experience is that a truly sacrificed life will receive all these things back again in new forms. It was said of Congreve after his death that 'like all truly mortified people he could take pleasure in simple comforts when affection put them his way' (see Mackay, 1918).

We now turn to the urgency of the task. The management speak of the modern church emphasizes burning platforms and the need for urgency (see, for example, Kotter, 2006). Many Catholic Anglicans find this uncomfortable because the Catholic senses a different source of urgency from those that are proposed. Urgency for the Catholic is in the prior work of God to call a soul to action, not in the immediate pressing need; it is vocational, not institutional. It is true that 97 per cent of the population don't worship; that the Church is institutionally vulnerable; that it is 80 times more likely for an 80-year-old to be in church than an 18-year-old; but these are 'secular' reasons for urgency. For the Catholic Anglican, urgency grows out of what Congreve (1910, p. 286) called 'the absorbing enthusiasm for God' that is a gift of grace. This means that there is no excuse for complacency in the suspicion of some of the reasons given for urgency, for the summons to mission is indeed urgent, though it is not urgent to save the Church, but enthusiastically to echo Christ: 'Repent, believe the gospel and come follow me.'

The context of Catholic mission

Anglican Catholics have often said that those who stand in other church traditions have it easier. Other traditions are variously thought of as serving richer places or more suburban communities or being less countercultural. Catholics, it is said, have all the back-street churches where no one else would go, the places with large populations that are actively of other faiths, the difficult mission fields.

In fact, Catholic Anglican churches can and do grow everywhere, and that should be the case, for the Catholic faith, the faith of the universal Church, is not something that only works in part of the world. The mission of the universal Church has a universal opportunity; as the psalmist wrote, 'The boundary lines have fallen for me in pleasant places; I have a goodly heritage' (Ps. 16.6).

The wider picture for mission in the United Kingdom is that the Church is back in the public domain. For good or ill, the views of the Archbishop of Canterbury about Amazon or Wonga are worth the news, and in many respects we 'do God'.[2] Individual churches and individual Christians may feel that we have little influence; but the Church is not without influence, and the exercise of adding up our various small pieces of influence is important to undertake.

In the diocese of London a few years ago we 'added up' to reveal the scale of our social action. Over 400 parishes engaged in more than 1,000 social action initiatives with 10,000 volunteers and 200,000 direct beneficiaries, raising and spending annually £17m – taken together, bigger than most charities in the UK.[3]

In Westminster, which is just one part of the archdeaconry of London, the Church offers to one of the biggest rough sleeping communities in the country two of the largest pieces and most effective responses in the form of the Connection at St Martin-in-the-Fields and the Church Army's Marylebone project for homeless women.[4]

It is not just in London that this is seen: 75 per cent of all rural schools are church schools, and the Church of England is otherwise a massive provider of education. Nor is this a matter just for dioceses and provinces: each parish or chaplaincy makes a contribution of volunteer hours that can be extraordinary when added up. An assessment of a community choir for a Heritage Lottery Grant revealed that this simple event released thousands of volunteer hours valued financially in tens of thousands of pounds. A tea for elders or open church day are contributions to local public life that are of inestimable worth, but they can, in the language of the world, also be monetized, added up and counted.

This is not done simply to justify a grant, but more profoundly and helpfully gives the Church credibility to be able to speak. It is a pre-evangelism upon which so much else depends. Such assessment supports other unexpected outcomes. We are beginning to see the openness of millennials and younger generations, whose rebellion is now away from the irreligion of their elders and towards things they see as helpful to the world – and in some instances to a church that is active in serving its neighbour in the name of Christ.

In every age new mission fields open; today, Facebook and Tripadvisor might be two. More and more churches find a means of mission in Tripadvisor, which is a tool used not just by tourists but by anyone coming new to an area. The award-winning Church of England Christmas social media campaign saw a 10 per cent increase in churchgoing on previous years.[5] The revamp of the Church Near You website is helping.[6] How are we equipping ourselves for this? There is less and less excuse for a ropey website and an absence from social media.

At the launch of the Church of England Alexa skill, the Bishop of Ely suggested that in a world of artificial intelligence Christian theologians have an important and relevant offer to make as people think again about what humanity is. Anselm's question *cur deus Homo?* has a new resonance and context in a world of artificial intelligence as we ask what it means to be human, which is a more profound and more fertile question than the questions of human sexuality requiring an anthropological understanding on which any answers will be dependent. The beginning of such thinking is happening around us as, for instance, Church of England schools begin their vision for education with the promise that Christ offers 'life in all its fullness'.

At this time there are global possibilities, and the question of how we are equipping those from overseas who come for a time to the UK to be evangelists when they return to their own nations becomes acute. If the oft-quoted but difficult-to-reference statement is true – that the 'average' (whatever that means) Anglican is an African woman under the age of 35 – the West is being re-evangelized from Africa. The challenge, then, is to be genuinely open to learn from zealous, faithful, committed Christians who seek to reawaken us to the joy of taking the gospel seriously.

There are always challenges in the mission field. Secularism is very strong. In the past we were intellectually incredible; now we are morally indefensible. Even those Christians who take a more liberal line on sexuality, gender and the rest are more conservative than secular society, let alone those of us who are more traditional. Moreover, the Church is in an environment in which the sins of the past, both active abuse and our failure to respond properly, all too often add up to re-abuse, thus curdling the relationships of the present. How the devil works to leverage evil …

Despite this, there is opportunity to speak effectively in our society. In order to find a language of mission it is necessary first to know what language society speaks, culturally and intellectually. Not so that the faith can be adapted to fit, but so that the faith can be articulated in a way that can be heard and understood.

That requires local embedding and response, and the tedious business of community audit. Too often the local church thinks it knows what it is doing, and that the landscape of the mission field is known. All too often, though, the mission field is changing and the missioners have not. How often is the Catholic Anglican, dazzled by the successes of the past, trying to be like a Victorian slum priest when the grotty flats have become million-pound lofts? Or in the centre of great cities, do we persist in serving middle-aged businesspeople on lunch breaks with truncated Masses set to fine music when in fact we should be reaching out to cleaners on night shifts and under-thirties working 60 hours a week? Knowing the context will enable appropriate and useful action in response to God's urgent call.

The tenets and methods of Catholic mission

The tenets of Catholic mission can be described as sacramental, pastoral and parochial.

In the face of Fresh Expressions of Church that don't prioritize or even celebrate a regular Mass, and churches in the evangelical tradition whose main Sunday service is often, even usually, a Service of the Word, Anglican Catholics are right to emphasize the centrality of the sacraments in the life of the Church. The sacraments are not a problem for mission, nor are they an aim to be worked towards once people have been evangelized, but they *are* the mission of the Church. Father Congreve taught that if mission flows from an entire focus on God, it must be sacramental because in the sacraments Christ himself is ministered, not simply ideas about him. Congreve wrote:

> Christ did not leave only a 'view', a 'philosophy'. If [he had], it is worth little more than any other philosophy. [But] If He gives himself in the sacraments of grace His religion is

Himself and is worth living and dying for. (Congreve, 1890–1917, pp. 99–100)

A focus on the sacraments means that we don't end up, as Congreve put it, 'picking out' from among the 'value systems' of religion 'the one best suited to improve the moral condition of the Heathens', which would be to reduce mission to 'a matter of tactics' (Congreve, 1910). This would, he said, be 'secular'. By contrast, Congreve taught that sacramental mission is specifically Christian, because it is founded on sacramental union with Christ.

This means that the very success of Christian mission depends on it being sacramental. Congreve asserts that results will come and souls will be brought to Christ if the missionary brings Christ himself sacramentally and not simply ideas and 'propaganda'. 'We can trust results, for in spite of European vices ... what we bring is God Himself and the results will be worthy of God' (Congreve, 1890–1917, pp. 99–100).

The question arises as to what sacramental mission actually involves. The parody is, like Father Ted, simply to say, 'I like a nice Mass'. Sacramental mission is not simply about putting on more services.

The conundrum of such a mission is that sacraments are by their nature bounded and reserved for the faithful. Father Damian Feeney has asked questions in his Sheffield lecture about the fences we put about the sacraments (Feeney, 2016). He challenged us to more open altars. Yet the caution of Michael Ramsey (Ramsey, 1957, p. 19) about everyone 'tripping to the altar' deserves to be heeded.[7] As Congreve noted, the Christian missioner brings the living God.

But you have come to Mount Zion and to the city of the living God, the heavenly Jerusalem, and to innumerable angels in festal gathering, and to the assembly of the firstborn who are enrolled in heaven, and to God the judge of all, and to the spirits of the righteous made perfect. (Heb. 12.22–23)

Start: Stop at St Stephen Walbrook is a service for those going to work – a service for which you are never early and never late. It allows people to start their day by stopping to reflect for 10 minutes. It has prayers and silence, music, Bible readings and a talk running once every 15 minutes for the two hours from 7.45 to 9.45 in the morning. It does not add to City workers' stress by demanding a fixed arrival time from a variable transport system, but rather enables prayer. There have been other experiments in a more Catholic mode – for instance, Exposition on Fleet Street, which ran for a time at St Dunstan-in-the-West for the crowds who go past each morning up Ludgate Hill.

Sacramental activity carries a duty of teaching because the literacy of the faith cannot be assumed. Eucharistic processions in Clerkenwell, and Marian ones in Kentish Town, have leaflets to explain what is going on to those who are attracted but uncomprehending of acts that witness to truths that have been forgotten or, more often, never learned.

Catholic Anglicans need to think how to take what is good from such initiatives as Ashes to Go and Anointing Points without reducing to advertising gimmicks sacraments that minister Christ personally to souls. Cleaning shoes on Maundy Thursday might be all right, but we have seen the madness of a decayed sacramentalism as bishops hand out cakes to commuters on the most solemn of all Fast Days.[8]

Our challenge in evangelizing with the sacraments is that they are offered but not belittled. Access cannot ever be a question of 'I want one of those'. Admission of young children to Holy Communion before confirmation is too often devoid of proper catechesis and genuine devotion and instead all about the inability of parents to say no to children, and of clergy to say no to harassed parents. Catholics in the Church of England must heed what Bonhoeffer said about 'cheap grace' and seek to *include* without *admitting* (Dowler, 2011, pp. 78–9, quoting Bonhoeffer, 1937).[9]

Part of this will be to find spaces for a catechumenate and

enable 'walking for confirmation' over a period as well as teaching about the sacraments in non-sacramental and non-traditional contexts. The discussion group in the coffee shop, the Bible Talk, the Guild meeting, the rosary group, might all be places where this can be done.

For Catholics the Church's year is sacral time, but we need flexibility if we are to be missional. Many years ago Bishop Lindsay Urwin said that in Advent there is the Church's time when we wear purple and wait while looking forward to the Parousia; and coterminously there is mission time when we have carol services galore, and Christmas activities – and teach what cannot be taught in Christmastide because it won't be heard.

It is amazing how many schools, secular groups, firms and other associations will respond to the offer of a carol service. In central London hundreds of thousands of people will attend carol services spread all through December. This is an opportunity not to be missed, to teach the incarnation, the starting point of all mission.

'Tumbling' from one moment in the year to another is a great help. At the secular concert of Christmas Music and Readings there is the advertisement of the Midnight Mass; and having got as many as possible to sign up to the Mailchimp at Christmas, some will come for more candlelight liturgy at Candlemas. Keeping the Christingle for Lent with a focus on the red ribbon representing the sacrifice of blood enables a deeper teaching which can be followed up with the invitation to Holy Week and Easter Day, and so on.

It helps to break events down into those that advertise, those that offer opportunities to observe, and those that invite participation. An advert event is anything that brings people through the door – for instance, a free children's activity or a concert of secular music. An activity morning for Advent or a concert of sacred music with a commentary to explain how the music is used in devotion are events that allow observation, looking without buying, coming without commitment. A liturgical performance of the music or a children's Mass using the frontal and Gospel Book cover made by the children, and the prayers written by them, are examples of events by which people might be moved through advert and observation to participation.

If Catholic mission is sacramental it is also usually said to be pastoral. The language of secular leadership manuals is viewed with suspicion, and the Good Shepherd is a model that is preferred by many Catholic Anglicans. To be pastoral in this sense is to be outward looking. It is not about gathering the elect and caring for the flock, but to be out on the hillside seeking the stray (Luke 15.4). Pastoral mission has aspects beyond the Church as well as within the fold.

Catholic Anglicans have prided themselves on the range and quality of their social action in the wider community. But a reminder is sometimes needed that Christian social action is not done to save the world: Jesus will do that, and the poor are always with us (Matt. 26.11). Christians are not politicians with less money and less power but those called to proclaim the love of Jesus in action.

The New Wine Churches are sometimes structured in missional communities. Rather than join the church and then join a small group, it is the shared endeavour of the missional community that creates 'sticky points' where people follow the vocation to service, joining the small group first, and then the church. Thus people are attracted to prison visiting; food banks; serving anonymous groups; advice work; debt counselling; memory cafés; lunch clubs, and so on.

None of these things are done because they help the Church to grow. Rather, they are a response to the call to love our neighbour. Social action does, however, help the Church to grow, and because we are acting with and for the Good Shepherd who is seeking the sheep, churches engaging in social action should organize activities so that growth is maximized. Some examples will help make this clear.

One charity invited City workers to donate suits in good condition so that job seekers could be well dressed for interviews, for which the charity also trained them. Based in a church building, it was not explicitly missional. Indeed, it was not thought right by the charity to take missional steps such as putting a prayer card in the inside pocket of each jacket or holding a thanksgiving service or embedding chaplaincy. The charity was so successful that it outgrew the church building, but the good work remained just that: a good work. It was not missional except in the most tangential sense.

Winter night shelters have by contrast been missional; not because they are proselytizing the vulnerable, but because volunteers have been drawn from congregations and have deepened in their faith. Many on the fringes of congregations have joined in and been led to a renewed or first devotion. At root this has been because the work has been sacramental, a participation in the disinterested love of Christ for his children. This love has been drawn forth by 'sacramentals' in the technical sense, activities that mediate grace, and emphasize the need to make sure, especially in a church making use of the missional community model, that these sacramentals remain central in the activity, and that prayers for the work, active engagement with other Christians, and scriptural reflection with an explicit focus on Christ are not lost.[10]

This implies leadership. Most Catholic Anglicans claim to use a pastoral model of leadership, but in reality the attitude in the tradition has been that the parish priest knows best, and Catholics have historically employed not a pastoral model but a *dictatorial* one. However, when this dictatorial model has been recognized, it is replaced by what is called a pastoral model, more collaborative and caring; but in fact it is all too often the dictatorial model done badly and with fewer results. In many ways the managerial model is better, and it can be genuinely pastoral.

This can be illustrated when considering visiting. It was always said, 'a house-going priest, a churchgoing people'. When my father died recently I found in his papers his visiting lists from 1951, carefully maintained. The job was to know everyone. The so-called Glass Ceiling theory states that a single pastor can manage about 153 people: the number in the miraculous draught of fish of John 20 (see Jackson and Piggott, 2010). To grow the local church in the old days you recruited mission women, more curates and so on, and they worked to bring in their 153.

In these days of thinner and more expensive human resources the leveraging of the numbers of pastors needs to be better done. Anglican Catholics have our own versions of those missional communities, each with its leader – guilds of visitors; the Mothers' Union; the youth group; the choir; men's and women's groups; Wednesday teas at the vicarage, and manifold other ways to structure the community. Good management ensures the church has an apparatus of record-keeping, welcome cards and follow-up visits. The parish priest may well not be able to know everyone. The crucial thing is not so much knowing people, but making sure that they are known.

All this is dependent on a well-trained and faithful laity, which means people need *managing*. The managerial things that help the work go smoothly – volunteer agreements, contracts, clear expectations, support, training – are pastoring. If done well then all the workers will be sharing – truly collaborating – with the mission that is led by the priest but effected by the people. For that task clergy are often not trained, so the challenge is to learn.

Managing can be hard. One church had a toddler group whose leader was not supported well enough in the faith by the priest. When some families joined (it was a 'sticky point') who said they did not want the prayers and the Bible story, it all began to drift. Good management and true pastoring was courage to close it down.

It helps that people should have a sense of membership. Catholics often hesitate over this: membership is by baptism. The Centenary Prayer Book produced 100 years after Keble's Assize Sermon said a good Catholic will show four notes of Catholic commitment; interestingly, they are just what the

Four Notes from New Wine say: regular worship; participation in catechesis; showing love of neighbour by joining in social action; financial giving – generously and from the moment of joining, not some months or years later (Church Literature Association, 1933).

For Catholic Anglicans the locus of all this has been the parish, which is 'the catholic unit'. Catholics approve parish inclusivism, contrast it with Fresh Expression particularism, and assert rightly that the Church is there in service of the community, not to offer chaplaincy to pools of believers. Care is needed in this. Certainly there is the charge of the cure of souls – but in real life when the Church gathers as the body of Christ it can seldom claim to be the whole community gathering or even a truly representative cross-section of it. Is this vision of the cure of souls of the whole parish not a chimera of the Parish Communion Movement or of an ideal village church?

Care is needed to avoid what we could call 'parish boundiarism': the parish is neither sacrament nor sacramental; it is the means by which we have a locus for deep community. When the Grenfell Tower fire happened, and elsewhere where there have been serious incidents, the work that had been done in the local churches over decades meant that they were known and had the contacts needed to offer what no one else could. This was a good in itself, but also great mission (see Plastow, 2018).

I chair the Faith Sector of London Resilience, the partnership board that coordinates the work of all those who respond to emergencies, and seeks to prevent them. Attitudes have shifted over recent years in the face of many similar responses to major and minor incidents. Whereas once emergency planners would query why there was a vicar in the room, they now ask, 'Why isn't there a vicar in the room?' Parish work, backed up by the wider strategic engagement that the Church of England enables, means that Anglicans can do Christendom. The result is the welcome back to the public square; the civic opportunity and duty that we have.

For all the parochial rhetoric, the caution is that the congregation in the parish church is so often a gathering of similar people, just as much as a church plant or Fresh Expression. How far are we made similar by coming together? How often do we say, 'Welcome to our church, it won't be long before you are just like us'? It helps to be 'just like us' since like will attract like; but the challenge is to have a number of different groups all meeting under the umbrella of the Catholic Church. The homogenous vision of the Parish Communion Movement of the Lord's People on the Lord's Day, all together as one at the Lord's Table, was not helpful – and possibly destroyed much.

Many have found that liturgies in different styles, at different times of the day and on different days of the week, have helped, and that events aimed at particular groups work well. What is the Walsingham Youth Pilgrimage if not a Fresh Expression aimed in a specific style at a particular group?

Catholic Anglicans can learn much from the 'non-parochial' church, many of which are in fact discoveries of Catholic life and practice by others who are reminding the Church of the treasures Catholics have perhaps rather neglected in a flight to the parish, but that would work so much better if they were again filled with Catholic devotion, used sacramentally and focused on personal holiness. There is much to gain from experimenting with new forms of church: interest groups; hot spots that focus activity in a specific place away from the parish church; forms of chaplaincy; work with schools; groups of parishes; forms of New Monasticism.

This is especially true of church planting. Catholics used to do it: most Anglican Catholic parishes started out as mission districts, daughter churches, and so on. The Catholic movement has fallen into the trap of evangelizing people to come to church but not to come to Mass. Thus if they move away they may fall away, and if they could help evangelize by moving to another church we cannot bear to lose them and they cannot bear to go.

Catholics have refused to listen when we are being told that when churches plant they grow, and we have believed we have not got the resources. There is much to say about planting, but we should not be afraid of this method; we should learn its grammar, which is not so far from that of the Catholic Church, and we should employ it.

Conclusion

In the end, all mission is God's mission. It begins with his grace in each one of us, for it is predicated on the outworking of the call to personal holiness. That is a result already attained; but it leads to results that can be measured, and the act of measuring, if done right, leads us to better action, for then we focus our activity, sacrifice self, and turn to God in what we do. This mission is good for the Church not because the institution is safeguarded, but because it is less without the contribution of those who are brought in.

Ours is a time of opportunity for mission, and for a Catholic mission that is sacramental, without belittling the sacraments; parochial, without preferring the parish to the kingdom of God; and pastoral, without denying the need to both lead and manage. We can be confident in embracing forms of mission that challenge us to a true diversity of activity and life. For this mission is God's mission, his gift to the world.

Notes

1 'To save my own soul is not to get something good for myself – but to give myself soul and body absolutely to the Creator for His love's sake to dispose of as He pleases' (Congreve, Letters to Friends and Associates 1890–1917 SSJE/6/5/2/6, f 98).

2 Alastair Campbell's remark, 'We don't do God', interrupting Prime Minister Tony Blair, was reported in the *Daily Telegraph* on 4 May 2003 (www.telegraph.co.uk/news/uknews/1429109/Campbell-interrupted-Blair-as-he-spoke-of-his-faith-We-dont-do-God.html).

3 For the Beyond Sundays Report, see www.london.anglican.org/articles/beyond-sundays/.

4 For the Connection, see www.connection-at-stmartins.org.uk/. For the St Marylebone Project, see www.churcharmy.org.uk/Groups/245011/Church_Army/ms/Marylebone_Project/About_Us/About_Us.aspx?redirected=1.

5 Ed Thornton (2018), 'Church of England digital team scoops five industry prizes', *Church Times*, 19 October, www.churchtimes.co.uk/articles/2018/19-october/news/uk/church-of-england-digital-team-scoops-five-industry-prizes (accessed 04/05/2020).

6 www.achurchnearyou.com/.

7 'The awe in the individual's approach to Holy Communion which characterized both the Tractarians and the Evangelicals of old stands in contrast to the ease with which our congregations come tripping to the altar week by week.'

8 The extraordinary success of Thy Kingdom Come 2019 on Trafalgar Square of the exposition of the Blessed Sacrament and the Confessionals are subsequent examples of good practice in this area.

9 Dowler quotes Bonhoeffer in the *Cost of Discipleship*, 1937: 'do we ... realize that this cheap grace has turned back upon us like a boomerang? The price we are having to pay today in the shape of the collapse of the organized church is only the inevitable consequence of our policy of making grace available to all at too low a cost. We gave away the word and sacraments wholesale, baptized, confirmed, and absolved a whole nation unasked and without condition. Our humanitarian sentiment made us give that which was holy to the scornful and unbelieving. We poured forth unending streams of grace. But the call to follow Jesus in the narrow way was hardly ever heard.'

10 Preaching at the profession of the first of the Sisters of the Holy Childhood, a teaching order in Oxford, Father George Congreve drew a distinction between the Religious House that is characterized by prayer and Rule, and thus is the 'Home of Jesus Christ', and 'a boarding house for church workers' (Congreve (1896), *Increase in us True Religion*, p. 11).

Bibliography

Bonhoeffer, Dietrich (1959), *The Cost of Discipleship*, second edn, London: SCM Press.

Church Literature Association (1933), *Centenary Prayer Book*, London: Church Literature Association.

Church of England (2005, 2019), SIAMS School Inspections, online at www.churchofengland.org/more/education-and-schools/church-schools-and-academies/siams-school-inspections.

Congreve, George (1874–1914), General Notebooks 1874–1914, Book 1, unpublished: catalogued in the Society of St John the Evangelist Archives, now held at Lambeth Palace, SSJE/6/5/3/19.

Congreve, George (1890–1917), Letters to Friends and Associates, unpublished, as previous reference, SSJE/6/5/2/6.

Congreve, George (1904), Meditation on the New Commandment, as previous reference, SSJE/6/5/3/10.

Congreve, George (1910), The Interior Life and Other Addresses, London: Macmillan.

Congreve, George (1913), Address to the East and West Missionary Society.

Dowler, Edward (2011), Theological Ethics, London: SCM Press.

Feeney, Damian (2016), Left in the Church: The 2016 Sheffield Lecture on Catholic Evangelism, online at https://damianfeeney.wordpress.com/2016/09/24/2016-sheffield-lecture-on-catholic-evangelism/.

Jackson, Bob and Alan Piggott (2010), Another Capital Idea: A Report for the Diocese of London, online at www.london.anglican.org/about/another-capital-idea/.

James, Serenhedd (2019), The Cowley Fathers, Norwich: Canterbury Press.

Kotter, John (2006), Our Iceberg is Melting, London: Macmillan.

Lewis, C. S. (1945), The Great Divorce, Glasgow and London: Geoffrey Bles.

Mackay, H. F. B. (1918), 'Funeral Sermon for Fr Congreve', published as 'Fr Congreve' in The Oxford Journal, May.

Plastow, John (2018), Mind the Gap: A Review of the Voluntary Sector Response to the Grenfell Tragedy, London: Muslim Aid, online at https://muslimaid.storage.googleapis.com/upload/www.muslimaid.org/media-centre/news/11-12-18_14-08-55_grenfell_report-cc_no_bleed%20%28copy%202%29.pdf.

Ramsey, Michael (1957), Durham Essays and Addresses, London: SPCK.

Sunde, Joseph (2016), 'The Halo Effect: The Economic Value of the Local Church', Acton Institute, 20 July, online at https://blog.acton.org/archives/88116-the-halo-effect-the-economic-value-of-the-local-church.html.

Wood-Daly, Michael (2016), Valuing Toronto's Faith Congregations, online at www.haloproject.ca/phase-1-toronto/.

Woodgate, M. V. (1956), Father Congreve of Cowley, London: Geoffrey Bles.

PART 2

Discussions

4

Reflections on Mary and Mission

PHILIP NORTH AND
GEMMA SIMMONDS CJ

PHILIP NORTH

Mary, Mother of Mission

While confidently a part of the Catholic tradition of Anglicanism, I am blessed to have many good friends from the evangelical wing of the Church. From time to time one or other of them will ask me to take them to the Holy House at Walsingham, keen to learn more about a place that plays such a big part in my own Christian life.

Now I know I should say yes with alacrity. I should be as keen as mustard to introduce them to the beauty of that holy place and the joys of knowing Mary as a companion on the way. I should put them in the car and drive them to England's Nazareth on the first available date.

The trouble is I don't do that. I agree in principle but then dither about dates, resisting concrete plans or diary comparisons. Why? Because I know that the moment that any of these friends sees the crowned image of Our Lady of Walsingham high above the Holy House altar, robed in cloth of gold and lit by the flickering tapers offered by devoted pilgrims, we will be at once re-fighting the battles of the Reformation.

My inner struggle symbolizes a problem for those of us in the Church of England who wish to give Mary a prominent place in our theology or spirituality. The still-weeping wounds of the Reformation give us a reticence when we are engaged with the wider Church, so Marian devotion becomes privatized, hidden away in Norfolk or pushed to the quieter corners of our parish churches.

Often we feel the need to defend our devotion to Mary against attack. We end up compromising with a relativist dialogue that accepts her as just about OK for those who are 'into that sort of thing' but certainly not part of the mainstream. We allow her to become an adjunct to the gospel rather than integral to it. Mary can all too easily be perceived as the after-dinner chocolates rather than the main course of the gospel meal.

The result of all this is that Mary can find herself reduced to being little more than a theological idea, stripped of her humanity. On the grounds that it is more acceptable to the mainstream of Anglicanism, we repeat the mantra that Mary's purpose is 'to point us to Jesus', which is of course true but lacks a certain richness, turning Mary into a signpost rather than a person in her own right. Newman's title for Mary as 'guarantor of the incarnation' is correct but rather cold, making the Mother of God sound like a part-player in a banking transaction. We can spend so much of our time defending Mary's place in the economy of our salvation against suspicion or attack that we forget that she is in fact a human being.

I want to speak, therefore, about Mary not as a theological idea, but as a person who by virtue of the resurrection is still alive. That means that we can be in contemporary relationship with her, one that is dynamic and mutual, and one that is related to – but also distinct from – the relationship we have with her son. I want to suggest that Mary is someone who inspires us in mission because we can love and know her personally.

I went on two pilgrimages recently. The first was the Youth Pilgrimage to Walsingham in which around 800 teenagers gathered together on a field outside the village for five days of pilgrim devotions and fellowship. Then a week later, I went on the Society of Mary Pilgrimage to Lourdes in the south of

France, again with a group, but this time comprising pilgrims of all ages.

In both cases the pilgrims were drawn primarily from the demographic groups with which the Church of England nationally most struggles to connect. They were almost all from urban parishes characterized by significant deprivation, large numbers were BAME, many of the younger pilgrims came from challenging family backgrounds, and a sizeable proportion were looked-after children. They were all united by a deep love for Mary. Not Mary as an idea or a theme or a metaphor, but Mary as a human being who they knew personally. There was nothing idolatrous about this love. In no way at all did it detract from the salvation that they found uniquely in her son as they shared in his saving work each day at the altar. But their love for Mary was genuine, sincere and dynamic. It was very beautiful to see, for example, tough black boys from estates one moment talking about their fear of knife crime and the next kneeling at the grotto to light a candle and pray.

And most interestingly for us, those pilgrimages were times of conversion. And by that I mean primary conversion in which people made a commitment to Christ for the first time in their lives. At the Youth Pilgrimage in particular I could tell of numerous instances in which, through relationship, teaching or sacramental encounter, young people have discovered the gospel for the first time, often then using the sacrament of confession as the moment when conversion is sealed.

The evidence of these pilgrimages, and many others, demonstrates that Mary is the model evangelist. She is incredibly good at making new Christians. Why is this? Let me suggest four reasons.

First, Mary shows us through her own life that it is in Christ that we find the *dignity of our humanity*. The lowly virgin of Nazareth shows that the beaten-up, the marginalized, the left-behind, and the disregarded are those in whom God invests his plan of salvation. She shows us that in Christ we can discover the beauty of our bodies and lives.

The doctrine of the Assumption is enlightening in this regard, a celebration that John MacQuarrie describes as 'one of the most humanistic of festivals' (MacQuarrie, 1990, p. 92). As Mary is assumed body and soul into heaven, so we see human life raised up to God by God in the culmination of the saving work of the incarnate Son. Through his body, our bodies are glorified, redeemed and raised up to heaven. In Mary, God shows us what we are all called to be – those whose bodies are redeemed through the incarnation.

Moreover, it is a female human life that is assumed, a female body in a culture in which the female body is so often objectified, sexualized and abused. That poses some challenges to us as Catholic Anglicans, especially in pointing out our failure to identify the central role that women, and especially women from poorer backgrounds, should be occupying in the Church's life. Those who accept the ordination of women think the issue is solved when it isn't (especially when our processes of vocational discernment structurally eliminate the poor). Those who cannot accept the ordination of women, but who still see the ministry and leadership of women as integral to the Church's life, are yet to give adequately imaginative answers to how those two viewpoints are reconciled.

In a world where one's dignity is usually contingent on one's wealth, where we still see vast structural injustices between people of different genders or ethnic backgrounds, and where many struggle to work out the goal or purpose of their lives, Mary shows us that it is in the saving work of her son that humanity finds its dignity and purpose. As she is set free in the Assumption, so she shows us the path of freedom.

Second, Mary *enriches our spiritual life* and so shows us how, in company with her, we can find relationship with God and then grow in the depth and the transforming power of that relationship.

Engaging in Anglican spirituality can require significant levels of literacy as you plot your way through books, seasons and lectionaries. This can make prayer in the Anglican tradition feel like a mental and intellectual exercise. People often presume that prayer is all about the individual bombarding God with words and intentions, whether spoken aloud or in one's head.

At a place of pilgrimage such as Lourdes you don't need an order of service, you don't need to be literate, you just need to be there. On a pilgrimage the worship is all-embracing and multi-sensual. The pilgrim is caught up in the life of a praying community with Mary as a companion and guide. It is easy to pray and so easy to grow in relationship with God.

A potent symbol of this is the rosary, which is the prayer of the poor, one that is rich and physical and pacey and meditative, but requires nothing other than the capacity to remember three well-known prayers. It works especially well with active teenagers because with its touch and movement it is prayer suited to a fidget-fingered generation. And of course the reason for the power of the rosary is that we are reminded constantly that we do not pray alone. Mary is our companion in prayer, our prayer partner, interceding powerfully with her son.

To pray is to be evangelized, for it is through prayer that our relationship with Jesus begins to develop and flourishes. It is through the depth of her own prayer life that Mary comes to know Jesus and then becomes the model evangelist for him, and so by praying with Mary we can deepen our relationship with her son.

Third, Mary shows us that *suffering has purpose*. Personal suffering is one of the great blocks in evangelism as those exploring faith can wonder where this God of love is when they are going through hard times. Again, here Mary can be an evangelist as she helps us to confront that question.

I remember as part of an outreach project taking the image of Our Lady of Walsingham to Aldershot Barracks during the Iraq war. We visited a parent and toddler group that was taking place in a community room at the barracks, attended by about 30 young mothers – none of whom had any Christian connection and most of whose husbands were away fighting in Iraq.

I spoke to them about the image of Mary standing at the foot of the cross. As a group of young women who were worried sick about their partners, they found this story to be an incredibly powerful one. Like them, Mary was desolate and stricken with anxiety about the one she loved but powerless to do anything to intervene. It is a potent image precisely because it does not provide easy answers. Mary simply stands in the place of suffering; she is just there. And often that is all we can do too – find the place where the cross is planted in our own lives and stand there and pray.

By growing in our love for Mary, we won't find that suffering is taken away. What we will find is one who suffered but who went on trusting and who eventually learned that all human suffering is redeemed in the resurrection of her Son.

And fourth, Mary is an evangelist because she *points to the joy of conversion*. And the important word here is joy. Of all the many titles that exist for Mary I think that my favourite is 'Cause of our joy'. Mary brings joy into the world through her 'yes' to the angel and through bearing in her womb the one who alone is our hope. Mary is also the one who delights with Elizabeth in the salvation that comes into the world through her child. This teenage girl, living in poverty, brought up in occupation, shows us the only source of lasting joy.

The gospel we proclaim is one of joy. We often forget this in an anxious Church, worried about decline, battered by scandals, anxious about its money and its buildings. The result is that congregations can become infected by anxiety and obsessed with the supposed glories of the past.

But the promise that Jesus makes to us is one of joy, a joy that awaits through his saving work on the cross but a joy that can be anticipated now in the sacramental life of the Church. Any congregation, no matter what size, can be a joyful one. And it is not our stress or anxiety that will bring people back to the Christ, but that joy which is his gift.

Mary can be a partner in joy. She is someone it is good to be with, good to know, good to love in her own right. For in our relationship with her we can be like Elizabeth, lost in shared joy at the conversion we find in her son.

In Mary, then, we see the supreme evangelist. As Anglicans we need to stop defending her place in the Church, denying her humanity, or hiding away our devotion to her. Instead we need to allow our relationship with her to grow in just the same way as we seek to build up our friendships with our fellow Christians. Mary walks with us on the way of Jesus. So as we build our relationship with her, our own ministry as evangelists can only be strengthened.

GEMMA SIMMONDS CJ

Hail, Mary ...

I don't remember a time when the mother of Jesus was not a member of our family. My French Catholic mother hung baptismal medals with her image on them around our baby necks. My convent primary school hymns spoke of her as a refuge for sinners. As a wild child, egged on by unruly older brothers, I frequently sought her refuge, though I found saying the rosary tedious. As I grew older I grew more critical of the soft colours and saccharine poses of statues and paintings and the sentimentality of many Marian hymns. The Latin of the *Salve Regina* offered a more satisfactory sense of a centuries-long tradition of prayer. The dark and quiet of the school's Lady Chapel often provided a place of refuge from wrathful teachers or prefects where I would sit telling the Mother of God my troubles. I took to saying the rosary as at least 'doing something' that felt like praying. The idea of a religious vocation, which had been hovering around me since I was small, began to take concrete shape, to my dismay and bewilderment. I found the long-winded Thirty Days Prayer in a book, with its promises of grace to be received, and in some desperation undertook to say it in hope of coming to a decision: 'take pity ... on my poverty and necessities; have compassion on my anxieties and cares; assist and comfort me ...' Mary's answer came, but took time to penetrate.

Around the same time my formidable Latin teacher, Lady Helen Asquith, every inch the granddaughter of a Prime Minister, one day told us of her annual trips to Lourdes. The idea that so towering a figure in my academic pantheon could go every year to serve the sick at the behest of Our Lady struck me forcibly, and aged 17 I found myself on a plane flying to Lourdes as a carer with a large group of severely ill and disabled people. I felt nervous being alongside sick people for the first time, but in prayer told Our Lady I would do anything she liked, as long as no one vomited anywhere near me – that was where I drew the line. Within an hour of arrival at the hospital someone had vomited comprehensively all over me. That was the last time I ever told the Mother of God that I was drawing a line. I now go to Lourdes every year as chaplain to a similar pilgrimage and have witnessed great miracles of personal healing. There is something about the baths at Lourdes that quite literally strips you down to the rock bottom of faith. As I am dunked into the bone-freezing water by the helpers I always feel overwhelmed by all the suffering around me, but also the faith and goodness, the longing for meaning of the sick and their young helpers. It is when my own sorrows and anxieties and wounds threaten to drown me, but where I have a sense that this is one place where I need to take them and leave them.

A period of missionary work in Brazil in the 1990s confronted me with Mary as mother of the poor, the forgotten and the persecuted of the world. The Magnificat became our great anthem of resistance and liberation. There I also found a Mary who became a major challenge to my worldview developed through university studies and a growing adult understanding of the position of women in the Church and in society. Her Magnificat tells of a God who subverts all abuses of power and patriarchy in the world and in the Church.

As theology and pastoral experience, personal journey and

intellectual struggles became more integrated, so the pious practices and Marian 'wallpaper' of my childhood solidified into something more gutsy and real, more challenging and more consoling at depth. Asked recently by the BBC to present the Sunday worship service on Mary for the week of prayer for Christian unity, I was able to bring all these elements into an explanation of the Marian dogmas and mysteries in light of our understanding of the mystery of the life, death and resurrection of Jesus. I came to a deeper realization that the more we pray with Mary, the more we gain an understanding of what it means to be a Spirit-filled human being. If we want to understand what it would mean to be full of grace, to respond with a deeply human, deeply godly generosity, vulnerability and openness to God's ways, we can find it in her own responses to the call she received. Mary is the archetypal disciple who shows in the mysteries of her own life what it means to be fully open to the power of the Spirit, manifest in the Son sent by the eternal Father. I ended the programme with 'My Fat Virgin Mary', a gloriously iconoclastic poem by Anglican priest Penelope Dent that echoes so much of where I am today as a thoroughly modern, deeply traditional Marian Catholic feminist.

'My Fat Virgin Mary'

I'm tired of skinny Virgin Marys,
Medieval, milk-mild.
The one I want has a bosom and a heart.
Brooding, maternal and magnificent.
You listen, you love
and you understand.
O most funny,
Glorious, vulgar fat lady.
I love you
and the God who made your
commodious bosom,

head rest, heart rest
for the uncomforted.
Hold us and love us,
you who dare to be big
  and despise corsets.
    You who love life
   and bottles of stout, pork pies and
   bags of greasy chips,
  wrapped in newspaper.
Belligerently beautiful,
Queen of all fat women,
Defender of the unloved.
Accuser of the small-minded, sawdust people,
who never get involved nor find the
time to love your son,
wrapped in themselves.
O most funny lady, most funny lady,
Mother of mothers,
Praise be to you for showing us your acceptance,
your grief and your rejoicing.
Praise be to you for daring to be big,
proud of your girth
and all Glorious within.

Penelope Dent (used with the author's permission)

Bibliography

MacQuarrie, John (1990), *Mary for All Christians*, Edinburgh: T & T Clark.

5

Reflections on Vocation and Mission

ANNA MATTHEWS AND ROBIN WARD

ANNA MATTHEWS

Shepherds or Saviours? Priesthood and Mission in the Church Today

> Priests are called to be servants and shepherds among the people to whom they are sent. (*Common Worship*, Ordination of Priests)

> We need missional priests, not pastoral priests. (An unnamed archdeacon)

> We are looking to appoint an influential and inspirational priest who will play a vital and strategic role in enhancing the governance, leadership and liturgical life of the church. (*Church Times* advert)

What are priests for? This may seem an odd place to start a talk about vocation and mission, for vocation encompasses all those Christ has made his own through baptism, and mission is certainly not the sole preserve of the clergy. Yet to ask what priests are for begs the further question: what is the Church for? And to ask what the Church is for brings us into the realm of mission, for if the Church is called to be a sign and foretaste of the kingdom of God, then the Church's job is to announce this good news, in word and action.

I used to think I knew what priests were for. Then I spent a little over six years as a Diocesan Director of Ordinands. At the end of this time, I felt less sure than I once had about what priests are believed to be for in the contemporary Church. The candidates I worked with came from across the breadth of the Church of England. They articulated their sense of vocation in different ways, and their expectations for the shape their ministry would take varied a lot. I worked with people passionate about leadership or growing the Church; those whose deepest desire was to help people grow in the knowledge and love of God; candidates whose commitment to helping the Church serve the poor and marginalized chastened and inspired me. I had pioneers who painted a picture of ministry that was creative and imaginative and, if I'm honest, slightly alarming for an Anglo-Catholic working with a fairly traditional model of priesthood. I had people drawn to the sort of multi-parish rural ministry that makes my heart thump in fear, and some ready and willing to make enormous sacrifices to follow God's call.

They were inspirational, a lot of them. They continue to give me hope. But I worried about them. What would the Church do to them, expect from them? What would happen to that passion and commitment and sacrifice and love? Would it be channelled in a way that would renew the Church and build up the Body of Christ? Or would the fire go out, the pressures of sustaining ministry in an anxious, over-stretched Church lead them to burn out or change direction, their initial call buried under the weight of other pressures and expectations?

I still don't know the answer to that, and it still worries me. What are priests for in today's Church of England? To sustain the institution? To keep the show on the road? To provide a gloss of spirituality or a glimpse of a deeper reality through the life events of a population for whom the gospel is now largely alien? Are priests there to invite people into the mystery and love of God and help them stay there and grow there? Or are we there to fundraise and manage building projects? To grow the Church? To find new ways of telling the story of a beauty ever ancient and ever new? To coordinate food banks and night shelters and debt counselling services to plug the gaps left by the state? To be the place of encounter with the crucified and risen Christ through whom we are drawn into relationship with the Father? All of the above? Some of the above? Other things than the above?

What priests are for relates very closely to what we think the Church is for – the Church is called, after all, to be a priestly people. And fundamentally the Church is not there to be a guardian of the nation's built heritage, or an adjunct to the social services, or even as chaplain to a community. The Church is there to announce, in its words and by its life, the reality of the kingdom of God. It is there to be a sign of the new creation, the place where we become sons and daughters of God by being drawn into Christ's life, and his perfect self-offering to the Father.

And that means that some things matter more than we often think or measure. The push for greater numbers of bums on pews has also to reckon with the sort of character a Christian community is called to show, the sorts of patterns of relationships in which healing, reconciliation, growth and holiness are learnt and practised and made visible. You can't do that so well in a mega-church where people don't know one another. You also can't do it in a small community closed off to anyone who isn't like the current members – a description that applies to more of our church communities than we often like to admit.

That the Church is called to be a sign of the new creation may very well – should – involve it in things like night shelters, food banks, debt counselling services, after-school clubs and dementia cafés. But, importantly, it is not doing this as a means of showing its relevance or gaining influence in a society that doesn't really know what to make of religion. It is doing it as a sign of the kingdom and its priorities, where the hungry are fed and the rich are sent away empty.

The Church needs this eschatological dimension to its life.

To be a sign of the new creation is to anticipate here and now the reconciliation of all things in Christ. And as we do that, as we learn to inhabit the space that Christ opens up for us, the Church becomes a gift, because it becomes a place where Christ continues to draw people to himself and make of them new creations. And in a world where polarization and division are so stark and threatening, do we not need the Church to remember this vocation?

Priests are there to attend to this reality, I think. To use the language of the ordinal, we are to be messengers, watchmen, and stewards of the Church. And that is what gives us our vocation and helps us understand our mission, which is God's mission. That's what sets the limits to the ways it's possible to reimagine priestly ministry, which isn't an infinitely elastic concept.

And if we are to be messengers, watchmen and watchwomen, and stewards of the reality of the new creation in Christ, we need first to have heard and received the message; to pay attention, and know how to discern the signs of new life; to honour and share the gifts entrusted to us.

We have to be open, first, to Christ's gift to us. Like Mary at the empty tomb, to know ourselves addressed by the risen Christ who calls each of us by name. And that's not something that happens once, where we receive our vocation and are sent off alone into the world to live it out. We need to keep returning, being drawn back to Christ, keep receiving his life as gift.

This is what will help us to resist others' fantasies that we are there as saviours – of people individually, or of the Church more generally. And it will also help us to resist our own fantasies that we are omnicompetent or indispensable, that we have everything sorted, or that we are justified by the busyness of our diaries or the offering of our own exhaustion.

To operate like that is worryingly easy, particularly in a church whose dominant climate is one of anxiety. It can be hard to sustain the priority of prayer and relationship with God when you're worried about numbers, stressed about the deficit in the budget, and feeling guilty for not engaging in yet another diocesan initiative. And that's before you've reckoned with the toll it's taken to sit with the couple whose baby has died, to anoint the parishioner afraid to die, to deal with the anger and grief of a congregation member who has almost reached the point of leaving the Church because of its multiple hypocrisies. Add to that all the routine stuff, and the desire to show your face at home often enough that your nearest and dearest remember who you are, and it's quite tempting to keep God at a distance. Sometimes the last thing we think we need, when it's hard enough to keep the plates spinning, is the unpredictable grace of the Holy Spirit.

And yet this is the grace that sustains God's new creation. This is the grace we are called both to receive and to minister. We need it. We depend on it. We can't be priests without it. St Bernard of Clairvaux, writing in the twelfth century, said this:

> The man who is wise, therefore, will see his life as more like a reservoir than a canal. The canal simultaneously pours out what it receives; the reservoir retains the water till it is filled, then discharges the overflow without loss to itself ... Today there are many in the Church who act like canals, the reservoirs are far too rare ... You too must learn to await this fullness before pouring out your gifts, do not try to be more generous than God. (*On the Song of Songs, Sermon 18*)

Do not try to be more generous than God. There is a freedom in that. It reminds us that we are finite; we need to hold on to this thought and to remember, even – especially – when we are representing the infinite God.

And it reminds us, invites us, to return to the source, to keep receiving the gifts of grace and new life. I meet quite a lot of clergy who pour themselves out for others and who are amazingly generous with themselves and their time; they who expend themselves while trying to help others grow in the knowledge and love of God, and feel guilty because they feel quite far from that knowledge and love themselves. I've been there too, and know what that feels like. And I know it's not sustainable in the long term.

And one of the things I tried to do with the ordination candidates I worked with, and still try to do with the clergy and ordinands who come to see me for spiritual direction or confession, is to help them hold on to – or recover – a sense of God's delight in them. St Augustine taught that good shepherds are made from good sheep, and that means that for those of us called to be servants and shepherds among the people to whom we are sent, we need first to hear the Good Shepherd calling us, to listen for his voice. If we are to nourish others we need first to let ourselves be fed, to seek nourishment in Scripture, sacrament and prayer. For as my spiritual director puts it, rather chillingly, hungry shepherds eat their sheep. If we are to search for God's children in the wilderness of the world's temptations, we need first to let ourselves be found, to let Christ heal and reconcile those parts of us that are lost or hurting, and to bring us home, rejoicing.

It's very easy to forget that we are the object of God's joy; that this is what he created us for. And even though I believe that, often I act as though God is somehow propitiated by the offering of my to-do list; as though I believe I can win his favour by showing him how busy (and therefore worthwhile) I am, as though somehow my exhaustion or stress is a sacrifice pleasing in his sight.

Time spent in the company of Christ reveals this for the nonsense and idolatry it is. God deals in truth, and he's not interested in sustaining my fantasies or allowing me to turn myself into a local saviour. God is interested in making me his, in drawing me alongside and into Christ, making me familiar enough with the contours and the topography of the new creation so I can help others navigate the way, and recognize the signs of God's presence around them. I can't do that when I'm so fixated on my own agenda that I pay no attention to the signs of grace; or when I have become so blinkered as a watchman that I miss the arrival of the God who often moves surprisingly.

Priests who can learn to be at home in the landscape of the new creation are missional priests. By their prayer, by their lives, by their words and actions, they point beyond themselves to Christ, and they help the Church to be more fully itself, which in turn helps the world to discern its vocation and identity as God's creation. By all means let them draw on the best of strategy, leadership and management. But let them not be so at home in that world that they neglect God's gifts of prayer, sacrament, Scripture and service, through which they remember who and whose they are.

ROBIN WARD

Being the Church: The Vocation of Mission

What is Catholic mission and vocation in the Church of England today? Catholics often feel as if they are flamingos in the Church of England zoo: picturesque, attractive to some of the visitors who like that sort of thing, probably worth some care and attention to conserve. But no one would want a whole zoo of flamingos, and if by some unfortunate accident – no doubt brought on by their rather needy attitudes – the flamingos were to die out, then they could probably be replaced just as well with more penguins. All too often Catholicism is treated as a standpoint that is looking for a place at the table, a 'spoon in the soup' as the former Bishop of London used to say. But the fundamental point about Catholicism is that it is not about being a party, it is about being the Church, and the Catholic Revival in the Church of England had as its inspiration from the beginning the doctrine of the Church, visible and ordered according to the formularies and liturgies contained in the Prayer Book, from which all the other revivals of ritual and devotion flowed.

So Catholic mission and vocation in the Church today,

expressed through a lived Catholic practice of the faith, has as its ambition not the preservation of a party or the cultivation of a particular rather rarefied cultural ethos. But those whose self-understanding is as Catholics within the Church of England do have a particular responsibility – as they have had since the Catholic Revival began – which is to draw attention to points of doctrine and spirituality that are in danger of being lost from the overall picture. That need is particularly acute today when for reasons of numerical and financial decline many of the ways in which the faith has been passed on are imperilled by a want of resources and a lack of formation. So, what are Catholic mission and vocation? What do Catholic Christians who are members of the Church of England have to say about mission and vocation that is distinctive as a contribution?

Two fundamental principles stand out. The objective ground for mission is the worship of God, the exercise of the virtue of religion which is so important in the theological vision of the foundational Anglican divine Richard Hooker, and the great point of continuity between the reformed settlement in England and what went before. The subjective ground for mission is the whole interlocking pattern of Christian practice that flows from the liturgical *terra firma* of Catholic life, and that forms individuals in conformity with the grace received in baptism: in short, parish ministry as ascetical theology.

Anglicans have never seen their churches and the communities that meet within them Sunday by Sunday as simply houses of instruction: convenient – or not so convenient – venues for religious pedagogy. Rather, the churches of England constitute a sacred landscape, in which the duty of worship that the commonwealth owes to God is fulfilled by the liturgical rites that are appointed to honour him. Hooker describes this thus: 'we have reason to think that all true virtues are to honour true religion as their parent, and all well-ordered commonweals to love her as their chiefest stay'.

But this isn't simply a point that depends for its force on Establishment, or on the sort of Christendom model of Christian public conformity that Hooker assumes. It is just as tangible and important in an environment that appears ever more hostile to Christianity and ever more disenchanted with the Cheshire-cat smile of a residual cult where it still lingers in the public sphere. The virtue of religion is not simply the discharge of a debt, albeit one owed to God himself. It is the organizing principle of our whole moral life, because as the German theologian Bernard Häring put it, 'our entire activity in the world must have a religious formation, for all our acts must be ordered to the loving majesty of God. This means that all our moral tasks are at the same time religious tasks.'

From this flows the fundamental outlook of Catholic mission. Worship, and in particular liturgical worship with the Eucharist at its summit, is not a weekly pedagogic top-up into which such Christian instruction as can be given in an hour's worth of communal activity is crammed, nor is it primarily a 'seeker friendly' exercise of welcome for potential new members of the gathering. Worship, Christian cult, is the work of Christ the High Priest, who alone offers perfect adoration to the Father, and through whom we offer worship as the priestly people of God only and solely because of our incorporation into him through our baptism. Liturgical worship – the sanctification of time through the Daily Office, the sanctification of human living through the rites and sacraments of initiation, confession, marriage, sickness and death, the sanctification of the Church as Bride of Christ through the mysterious two-fold consecration, sacrifice and communion of the Eucharist – is a real 'enrolment' of the people of God, giving form and substance to their moral and spiritual life in Christ.

The Catholic Revival in the Church of England had the good fortune to coincide with the cultural and artistic self-confidence of the romantic movement, particularly the gothic revival. The Oxford Movement is sometimes represented as a high-minded and austere theological project that was trivialized and made polemical by the second generation of ritualists. Nothing could be further from the truth. Not just in England, but across Europe, the ravages of the revolutionary wars were put right with the help of a religious sensibility that saw the beauty of holiness as its primary engine of evangelization. This is apparent in sacred art, in literature, and in the renewed sense of the sacred that informs almost every detail of the vast project of catechesis and conversion that characterizes the nineteenth-century revival from Solesmes to Cowley. The extraordinary potency of Notre Dame de Paris as a symbol and custodian of the city's identity and pride following the fire of 2019 is a telling reminder of how effective this project was, how deeply it lodged in the spirit of even an avowedly secular state, and how much the cathedral still evokes a sense of the sacred. Indeed, the incredulous reaction in the British media that so much money could be raised so quickly for what was apparently only understood here as a 'heritage' issue indicates that the sort of inchoate religious affiliation that the fire made apparent is not at all dependent on the sort of tepid official religiosity that survives here.

But as Michel Houellebecq made clear in his prescient 2015 novel *Soumission*, the way through to belief supplied by this rich culture is no longer straightforward. The protagonist of the novel is an academic expert on Huysmans, the high priest of Catholic aestheticism and of the Notre Dame cult in particular. But shaken out of a life of nihilistic routine, he finds himself unable to connect with his subject's spirituality, a moment captured by Houellebecq by the smoke detector the academic finds in his monastery cell. There is a malaise about contemporary Catholic culture, and that malaise is particularly apparent in the way our liturgical aspirations fail to match up to the evangelistic impetus that is meant to inspire them.

Ever since the mid-1960s, and particularly in the liturgical ethos inspired by the implementation of the liturgical reform ordered by the Second Vatican Council and carried out with great speed in the five years that followed its end, Catholics have been asked to emphasize in the rites of the Church simplicity, intelligibility, and a demotic ethos that avoids the sense of pomp and formality that the culture of Europe inherited from the Romans. At the time of the Council this was identified as being necessary if three groups of people were to be successfully evangelized in the coming years: the working class of Europe; the newly liberated colonial peoples of Asia and Africa; and the Christians living under communist rule who were deprived of any non-liturgical catechesis.

These principles were very largely accepted by Anglican Catholics, so that by the 1980s any sort of attachment to the previous liturgical forms, in particular the celebration of the Eucharist at anything but a 'forward-facing' altar, or the traditional chant of the Church, was seen as retrograde and excluded from seminaries and parishes. But it is now evident that this has been largely a failed experiment. Whereas the richer, more complex and even abstruse rites that arose as missional innovations in the Anglicanism of the nineteenth century proved transformative of the Church of England's ethos and self-understanding, the newer, more accessible versions have produced a cultural malaise and a sense of boredom in the liturgy, in which bathos and the didacticism of the school-room have replaced a rich cultic resonance and mystagogy.

All too often, Anglican parishes in the Catholic tradition are still wedded to a liturgical ethos in which a small group of people gather around a forward-facing altar often intruded into a building for which it is particularly ill-suited, singing music that might once have been energizing in a straightforward way for a congregation of 150 but is enervating and depressing for 30. This inevitably exacerbates the sense of bereavement that dwindling congregations have to confront, and even fails in what it was most intended to promote, when catechesis has to struggle with excessively long scriptural readings read in flat and unmemorable translations. Moreover, this liturgical ethos is heavily clericalized, so that the shortcomings of the clergy that were once constrained by the precepts of the rite now run amok through the rubrical and ceremonial choices provided.

One of the key reforms needed, therefore, to reinvigorate Catholic mission in the Church of England is to look again at the liturgy. It can be no surprise that in a Church where lightly liturgical charismatic evangelical sensibilities are now the norm, those in positions of leadership from that tradition see little reason to sustain diminishing parishes of a Catholic outlook when the worship that takes place in them seems incapable of sustaining much of an evangelistic life. Here the liturgical theology of Pope Benedict XVI is of crucial importance, coming as it does out of a pastoral and ecclesial perspective, and complementing the sort of insights that have been expressed in an English-speaking context by scholars such as Catherine Pickstock and Margaret Barker. This is a manifesto for resacralization: overly didactic flattening of liturgical rites, the exclusion of the sort of resonance that comes from apparent redundancies and repetitions and obscuries in ritual and text – even with the good motive of forwarding 'active participation' – have produced a contemporary liturgical idiom that seems in many fundamental respects to be much less able to transmit and sustain the faith than did the rites they replaced in the 1960s.

This objective reform is essential if the subjective ground for mission in the Catholic tradition – the practice of parish ministry as ascetical theology – is to have any sort of revivifying energy for people. It is not difficult to see when comparing what used to be published to sustain lay spirituality in the Catholic tradition with what is published now how thin a diet is available to the Christian living out a lay vocation in the world. This begins with the Babel-like confusion and complexity of modern liturgical texts, particularly for the Daily Office, which compel users to employ multiple volumes and mark myriad places in them just to say the most elementary versions of morning and evening prayers. To a degree, telephone apps help with this, but not when people attempt to build up a liturgical community of prayer with others, perhaps in their parish churches or perhaps in a work setting.

Moreover, there is a real paucity of spiritual publishing, for the laity in particular, that will sustain the sort of serious spiritual regimen that the last significant Anglican Catholic writer on parochial ascetics, Martin Thornton, thought characteristic and necessary. Again, here the internet has brought a lot of improvement, as texts can be scanned and published online and secondhand books bought much more easily. But the decline in religious communities, and so in the number of people able and competent to deliver retreats and give missions in parishes, means that many Christians lack any sort of encounter with those who have a particular expertise in communicating spiritual practices. Left to their own devices, even relatively straightforward endeavours like making an appropriate Rule of Life become problematic, and the sort of ascetic superstructure that was once readily available to lay people in particular and taught consistently in parishes has largely disappeared, to be replaced with a much more haphazard concept of the spiritual life, unhappily combined with an assumption that receiving Holy Communion requires no particular preparation or self-examination each week.

One of the reasons for this malaise is a sacramental hiatus that has grown up in the Church of England, particularly in relation to confirmation and confession. Confirmation is a rite and a sacrament in grave decline: when I was an incumbent in the diocese of Rochester 15 years ago the bishop wrote to all the clergy admonishing us when the number of confirmations fell below 1,000 a year. There are now about 400. In the diocese of Gloucester there were 70 confirmation candidates in 2017, a number that in the past would have been accounted for by one decent school confirmation service. In fact, without the confirmation services still held regularly in public schools, there would be precious few candidates at all. Does this matter? The Church in Wales has recently decided not, by declaring Christian initiation to be complete in baptism. This position was vigorously resisted by Anglican Catholics in the heyday of the Oxford Movement, most notably by Gregory Dix and

Lionel Thornton, who understood what an important station in the life of grace confirmation imparted.

As with confirmation, so with confession. I recently had a conversation with a retired bishop who told me that when he was serving his title in the early 1970s the parish was considered a moderately Catholic one – no incense, no Marian devotion. But there was a daily celebration of Holy Communion, well supported, and he was expected to be available to hear confessions on a weekly basis in church once he became a priest. People understood what confession was about and used it. Now it seems from the discussion about abolishing the sacramental seal that confession is seen as the preserve of the most advanced Anglo-Catholics left in the Church of England, an impediment to effective safeguarding and a legal anomaly with adverse consequences for insurers. This is hugely corrosive for Catholic mission and the discernment that people need for choosing their vocation in life: no one witnessing the way in which the faith of young people and their life choices are strengthened by the hearing of confessions at the Walsingham youth pilgrimage could imagine that the practice of making a sacramental confession is an obstacle to spiritual growth.

What can be done about this? One important way is to ensure that the clergy are given a more thorough training in ascetic theology, something that on the whole American Episcopal seminaries have done better than us. Here the work of the late Martin Thornton is worth reconsidering: work that has become unfortunately associated, through his use of the word 'remnant', with a passive acceptance of numerical decline. Thornton realized that spiritual training was the principal duty of the parish clergy, and that to do it well required active lay supporters and a systematic knowledge of the spiritual practices that effective use of the Church's liturgy presupposed. Without this grounding, clergy are exposed to an essentially eclectic working out of their vocation, one that is impressionistic, unstable and, in the end, ineffective. One of the reasons why religious vocations have declined so precipitously in the

Western Church is the way in which well-intentioned attempts to refresh the charism of existing orders have simply left people vowed to a life that no longer exists, and re-deployed to one for which they are simply not suited.

The Catholic Revival in the Church of England was, above all, confident. The Oxford Fathers were realistic about the degree to which the Church of England understood itself as Protestant, unsacramental, and opposed to enthusiasm in matters of religion. But they thought that the Prayer Book and the formularies of the Church provided a strong enough basis on which to go forward, and wove around them a rich and fruitful doctrinal, spiritual and artistic synthesis that completely transformed the Church. Like many Anglican Christians today in England, we can experience this success as a bereavement: what has become of all this, especially when we find ourselves surrounded by so much of the material culture of this world, seemingly ever more bereft of meaning? But Catholic mission in the Church of England – precisely because it is Catholic and not insular – will always be able to draw on sources of revival broader than itself.

Here, then, we need to think about how significant developments in world Catholicism are reinvigorating mission. In particular, the revival in traditional liturgical forms, which has often been greeted in the past with a paranoid fury by those in authority, had moved well beyond antiquarianism and a grudging concession to the pastoral needs of the elderly, and is now a young movement resourced effectively by the internet. We need to hear this, and see it in action, especially in communities such as Pusey House in Oxford where thorough vocational formation is carried out in a fulsome and demanding liturgical setting. And we need to have confidence in the ascetical integrity of Catholic living, in which the force of the sacramental life extends throughout the possibilities of virtuous living, as St Thomas Aquinas set out with such insight and clarity. So will the providence of God mercifully add to those called to the household of faith.

6

Reflections on the Sacraments as Converting Ordinances

DAMIAN FEENEY

How can sacraments convert? To begin with, they are channels of grace – the gift of God to his people. Conversations about the nature of evangelism, prone to displacement discussions about strategy, models and case studies, ultimately reach the shore of understanding that 'God is the Evangelist'. That is to say, the very business of evangelization is one in which human decisions about evangelistic strategy and implementation are secondary to the primary urge – the dynamic outpouring of grace that is part of the fundamental nature of God, and the willingness of communities and individuals to discern the direction of that urge. The gift of conversion is thus part of the grace that is God's gift. The sacraments of Baptism and Eucharist embody this sense most obviously, but it may be argued that the whole sacramental economy is in fact charged with the task of bringing the grace of conversion into the lives of individuals and communities. In other words, the relationship between the Church and the world is ordered by a sacramental view, in terms of both recognized sacraments and a wider sacramentality that is part of the natural order.

The unhelpful polarizations that beset a Church encompassing a variety of traditions and beliefs have led in some measure to the downplaying of this ethos. Proclamation is a verbal, oral act, it could be argued, and conversion takes place through verbal witness, testimony and the making known of the grace and glory of God to those who have never viewed the world through the insights of Christian revelation. Nothing I am saying contradicts any of this. Rather, such witness is at its most effective if it is transmitted in a context where sacraments are recognized as having their proper place in a balanced understanding of proclamation. Our faith has never been, can never be, 'all talk'. Witness takes its form in several ways – the proclamation of liturgy; the worship, which speaks of God's mercy and forgiveness; the acts that speak of divine healing and restoration. Furthermore (and vitally) the liturgy acts as a springboard from which the believer is sent out to witness to the truth of belief through acts of service, love, forgiveness and compassion. This is the crucial, axiomatic connection that determines whether Christian worship is in fact witness at all.

Our understanding of conversion seldom seems to refer to the context of the Church – who and what we believe the Church to be, and the nature of the core, defining reality of the sacramental nature of the Church in Christian witness. The witness, as it were, of the sacraments of the Church gives a real context for the proclamation of the good news of Jesus Christ. In addition, the multi-faceted sacramental ethos – whether from the point of view of the different types of encounter with God, or the many aspects of the grace received – means that there is a rich diet of understanding and relationship available to the faithful soul. To see sacraments as converting ordinances reinforces our understanding of who and what the Church is, and encourages an appropriate understanding of the Church as the body of Christ: the community in which we discover, and gather around, the risen Jesus.

Sacraments as signs of relationship

Henri de Lubac develops the sacramental analogy that intimately relates God, Christ and Church:

Christ is the sacrament of God, the Church is ... the sacrament of Christ; she represents him, she really makes him present. She not only carries on his work, but she is his very continuation, in a sense far more real than that in which it can be said that any human institution is its founder's continuation. (de Lubac, 1950, p. 29)

So, the relationship between God, Christ and the Church is a sacramental one. Indeed, the Church is the very continuation of the incarnate life of Jesus Christ, and is so through an understanding and series of relationships that are sacramental in ethos and fundamental expression. The multi-faceted nature of sacraments means that a message so expressed moves beyond the purely verbal, engaging all the senses and stressing the importance of community as the context in which witness is lived and proclaimed.

The connection between evangelism and liturgy

Recognizing that evangelism is not merely an activity happening at one remove from the Church has serious implications both for the work of the evangelist and for the witnessing community in general. Popular perceptions of the evangelist working at the 'edge' of worshipping communities are balanced by the direction of travel and the understanding that what is to be found in such communities are themselves integral to the dynamic of conversion. This is further reinforced by the nature of worshipping communities themselves. All might be said to be on an ongoing journey of discovery and encounter, and faith is something that deepens over time. The community in this sense is very far from the finished article, far from fully converted to discipleship in Jesus Christ. Sacraments are a major part of the means by which Christians journey on through new insights that challenge, encourage and persuade to a deeper relationship with God, and the amendment of life that is integral to that relationship. Conversion is seldom, if ever, a one-off moment of revelation and discovery, but is a dynamic, taking place over time.

All of this is summarized by Ratzinger, who recognizes sacraments as 'the fulfilment of the life of the church', and thus not merely individual concepts, acts or events with no relationship to the being of the whole Church. He further points to sacraments as *communal* events, and as such are indicative of the wider question of the unity of all humanity. Finally, he draws together the issues of human togetherness and union with God.

> the Church is not merely an external society of believers; by her nature, she is a liturgical community; she is most truly Church when she celebrates the Eucharist and makes present the redemptive love of Jesus Christ. (Ratzinger, 1987, p. 50)

Ratzinger's view is not merely restricted to a view of the Eucharist as representative of the fullness of the Church's expression. Because the Church is *communion*, Church and Eucharist are one and the same:

> she (the Church) is God's communing with men in Christ and hence the communing of men with one another – and, in consequence, sacrament, sign, instrument of salvation. The Church is the celebration of the Eucharist; the Eucharist is the Church; they do not simply stand side by side; they are one and the same. The Eucharist is the *sacramentum Christi* and, because the Church is *Eucharistia*, she is therefore also *sacramentum* – the sacrament to which all the other sacraments are ordered. (Ratzinger, 1987, p. 53)

Flowing, therefore, from a view of church in which mission is received, and of which the Church itself is the fullest expression, comes a sense of the identity of the Church being most fully and faithfully expressed within the sacramental relationship between God, Christ and Church. Sacramentality is not merely an emphasis or a preference; rather, it is essential as an expression of the nature of the Church; without it, the Church ceases to be the Church.

It is in the writings of von Balthasar that the intimacy of relationship between Christ, Church and Eucharist attains its greatest depth. In addressing the question as to why Christ did not complete his unique mission, leaving it to the Holy Spirit and Church, Healy and Schindler (2004, p. 56) point to a three-stage argument in von Balthasar's writing. First, an appeal to the patristic notion 'that which has not been assumed cannot be restored' (Gregory of Nazianzus, Epistle 101) reminds us that Christ's death was necessary to redeem the death of other humans. Second, Christ's death is the high point of the revelation of infinite love, and is the moment of the handing over of the Spirit. Third, the constant presence of the Spirit throughout the incarnation points to the Eucharistic 'universalization' as something not alien to Christ, but a gift that is enabled through his relationship to the Holy Spirit and the Church:

> There can be nothing of the Spirit in the Church that does not coincide with Christ's reality, christologically, that does not let itself be translated into the language of the Eucharist – the surrender of Christ's own flesh and blood. (von Balthasar, 1995, pp. 237–8)

In articulating this principle further, Healy and Schindler reinforce von Balthasar's principle of 'life-giving exchange', offering a descriptive and compelling insight from which the missiological significance of the Eucharist flows. The principal points here are that the Church is born with Christ's death, and present beneath the cross to receive it.

This is why the theological tradition has always understood the true birth of the Church as symbolized by the blood and water coming from the pierced side of Christ, the new Adam, from whose side comes the new Eve. In the person of Mary, the Church is also present at the foot of the cross to receive the gift communicated by Christ. The Church is both the body and blood of Christ poured out for the salvation of the world and the bride who, in receiving the substance of Christ's life in the Eucharist, brings new life to the world (Healy and Schindler, 2004, p. 57).

The birth of the Church is therefore an event, an action, in a specific place and time. It has a given particularity and tangibility that is rendered more explicit, more particular still, by the Eucharist which it fulfils and which flows from it. Here, the explicit and intimate Eucharistic ecclesiology offered by von Balthasar stands in stark contrast to much contemporary mission activity in the field of Fresh Expressions. The Church cannot relegate or sublimate the Eucharist. It is difficult to imagine a practical scenario in which a body that begins with no sacramental expression or clear understanding of how the Eucharist is to be expressed can incorporate the Eucharist subsequently in such a way that it becomes the core, defining activity, the perceived end of all mission activity, and the place where the world will find itself as the Church pours itself out for the life of that world.

What of the 'non-participant'?

This in turn leads to a further question raised by the use of the Eucharist as a core evangelistic medium – the question concerning those who are not fully incorporated into the Eucharistic life of the worshipping. This question is implied by Dulles, who asks:

> Does the grace of Christ operate beyond the borders of the visible Church? What could this mean? If the Church is defined as the visible sacrament of Christ's invisible grace, the question may be rephrased to read: Can the grace of Christ

be present and operative and yet fail to reach its appropriate corporate expression? (Dulles, 2002, p. 71)

Clearly this question has profound implications for any understanding of the role of the Eucharist as an evangelistic action. Is the grace inherent in sacramental action accessible or capable of being encountered by non-participant spectators? Dulles makes general statements here concerning God's love for all, and states that others besides Christians are recipients of grace. This is coupled with a reminder that the Church is never fully the Church in this world in any case. Nevertheless, Dulles is clear in his understanding that 'others besides Christians are recipients of God's grace in Christ':

> When the Church is present, celebrating the Eucharist, she is the unique sacrament of Christ, who is in turn the Sacrament of God. The grace which emanates from this encounter can be received both by those who are fully incorporated into the life of the church and those who are not. (Dulles, 2002, p. 71)

In addition, there is a key theological question concerning the nature of what might be called 'Eucharistic Evangelism'. If Jesus is truly present and encountered through this supreme mystery, and if the purpose of evangelism concerns the processes whereby we are drawn closer to Christ (whether word-based or otherwise), then this presupposes that the Eucharist is – or ought to be – central to evangelism. The papal encyclical *Evangelii Nuntiandi* (Paul VI, 1975, p. 58) makes explicit the relationship between Christ, Church and evangelization, with the Eucharist at its heart:

> The preaching ... of the search for God Himself through prayer which is principally that of adoration and thanksgiving, but also through communion with the visible sign of the encounter with God which is the Church of Jesus Christ; and this communion in its turn is expressed by the appli-

cation of those other signs of Christ living and acting in the Church which are the sacraments. To live the sacraments in this way, bringing their celebration to a true fullness, is not ... to impede or to accept a distortion of evangelization: it is rather to complete it. For in its totality, evangelization – over and above the preaching of a message – consists in the implantation of the Church, which does not exist without the driving force which is the sacramental life culminating in the Eucharist.

Although the encyclical speaks here of the Eucharist as a *culmination* of evangelization, the language employed is none the less interesting. The totality of evangelization consists in the *implantation* of the Church, itself dependent on its sacramentality. The implication that the whole process of evangelization is dependent upon that inherent sacramentality cannot be avoided.

Baptism as a gateway and a challenge

Perhaps it is in the sacrament of Holy Baptism that the greatest potential, and yet the greatest frustration, is discovered. This sacrament is still sought by many families with young children, despite a merely sketchy understanding of the rigour and future life that is heavily suggested by the liturgy. Promises of faithfulness, of turning away from evil, and turning to Christ, can end up being profoundly undervalued, misunderstood, and passed over, and the liturgy becomes an arcane one, devoid of deeper meaning for those present. But the actual event rarely fails to make an impression, and the effect of the rite, with its powerful signposts, and the combination of spoken and enacted truth, makes its mark. The same is often true for those who witness the rite of confirmation and ordination, as the witness and example of candidates (frequently to those who are closest to them) leads to inevitable personal questioning.

The development to encourage this questioning, and to offer the ministries by which feelings can be explored, is a welcome step forward on these 'set piece' occasions. There is an instinctive sense that these rites speak powerfully, very often to those with little or no faith background.

Of course, such rites are foundational to those who through them are incorporated into the body of Christ, and challenges the sense that sacraments are there merely for those who are already in some sense incorporated into the institution. It is easy to decry the notion of certain sacraments as 'rites of passage', and yet this is a clear marking out of the Christian journey from cradle to grave, appropriate for different stages of enquiry and maturity. This is particularly true of the sacrament of Holy Matrimony, in which grace flows through the words and actions of the couple themselves, and where the task of the Church is to witness, to bless and to rejoice. Once again it is a fruitful exercise to remind ourselves that grace extends beyond the direct recipients, as the overflowing of joy and the challenges to faithful living are outlined both verbally and non-verbally, and themselves are capable of playing a part in conversion.

Reception, and the nature of participation

One question that lingers in our understanding of sacramental conversion concerns Eucharistic reception, often cited as an issue in considering sacramental life as that around which evangelism and conversion happens. Experience of Eucharistic church plants in public places begs the question 'Who may receive?' This question can be painted as a classic conundrum between the institutional needs of the Church and the missiological priorities of a given context, and the issue can founder on notions of inclusivity. In some cases, a policy of open reception, while contrary to the practice of the Church, has been used as a means by which others could be drawn more readily into the worshipping body. Urwin, himself an Anglican bishop, reflects upon the experiences of applying the norms of Anglican sacramental practice in an overtly mission context thus:

> I acknowledge that this open table approach is contrary to Anglican teaching. It is an exception, and my fragile judgement on that occasion was that I was not responsible for anyone eating and drinking condemnation to themselves – a serious matter indeed in the writings of Paul. Perhaps I will have the opportunity to baptise someone who received the bread and wine on that day (in the wrong order) just because they had been invited to eat. (Urwin, 2008, p. 39)

This pattern certainly runs counter to the practice of the early Church, in which admission to the full mysteries of the Eucharist was possible only after full rites of initiation, which make much current praxis seem vague and half-hearted by comparison. In addition, this practice has a mythologizing effect that has shaped many attitudes. This is a point reinforced by Tilby, who describes

> a firm boundary beyond which the general enquirer or fellow traveller could not go without a personal willingness to submit to the disciplines of the life of the Body itself. (Tilby, 2008, pp. 87–8)

Within the Church of England it has been the traditional practice to admit to communion those who have received the full initiation implied by the sacraments of Baptism and Confirmation. A whole variety of reasons are offered for this, as well as ways being sought to render this more flexible in appropriate pastoral circumstances. The advice from the House of Bishops allowing permission to be given for reception to communion of those 'desirous of being confirmed' is one such example, but it is unhelpful to those who may be baptized as infants, but not yet confirmed (for whatever reason). There is a real need here for wise and contextualized missiology in practice, and careful planning concerning rites of initiation and incorporation. Of course, the altar rail, or other point of reception, is never the place to ask questions concerning baptismal status, and the preferred instinct in cases of uncertainty should be to enable reception. Without this, the potent message of hospitality and inclusive grace is thwarted as what is stated in words is then not acted upon.

Dulles's view of grace operating outside the body does not limit itself simply to those who receive the sacrament. Such grace is open to all, since God is the loving Father of all, and his redemptive love is available to all (Dulles, 2002, p. 63). To be a bystander at the sacramental event is therefore to be available to that grace. This may well challenge our understanding of 'participation' in a liturgical context, and lead us to a refreshed view of what sacraments are and how they operate.

Tangibility

Sacraments use physical, tangible things in order to convey the deep mysteries in which they participate: water, oil, bread, wine. This sense of the need for tangible expression is stressed in *Sacrosanctum Consilium* (para.7), which describes the liturgy as 'the presentation of man's sanctification under the guise of signs perceptible to the senses'. These statements make a strong argument for the need for the physical and the tangible in the dialogic world of worship. Within this material economy the language of giving and receiving is inextricably linked with the language of covenant, upon which the Christian community relies in its dealings with God. Furthermore, this understanding of the tangible and the need for covenant exchange is deeply resonant with, and indicative of, incarnation – the very *material* nature of the Word-made-Flesh. All this is summed up in the memorable words of Rahner:

Essentially the Church is the historically continuing presence of the incarnate Word of God. She is the historical tangibility of the salvific will of God as revealed in Christ. Therefore the Church is most tangibly and intensively an 'event' where (through the words of consecration) Christ himself is present in his own congregation as the crucified and resurrected Saviour, the fount of salvation: where the Redemption makes itself *felt* in the congregation by becoming sacramentally visible; where the 'New and Eternal Testament' which he founded on the cross is most palpably and actually present in the holy remembrance of its first institution. (Rahner, 1963, p. 317)

Conclusion

In arguing for a renewed understanding of the importance of the sacramental economy within the missional life of the Church, I am conscious that much work remains to be done in fully exploring the theology that links together our understandings of liturgy, community and sacramental grace, and that in the 'mixed economy' of Anglicanism it can be both fruitful and difficult to bring different traditions of Catholic and reformed theology into genuine and creative coherence. To travel this road, however, would be to unlock the sacred mysteries still further as converting ordinances, and that, surely, makes the journey worthwhile.

Bibliography

Croft, S. (ed.) (2008), *Mission-shaped Questions*, London: Church House Publishing.

De Lubac, H. (1950), *Catholicism*, London: Burns, Oates and Washbourne.

Dulles, A. (2002), *Models of the Church*, New York: Doubleday.

Healy, N. and D. L. Schindler (2004), in *The Cambridge Companion to Hans Urs von Balthasar*, Cambridge: Cambridge University Press.

Paul VI (1975), *Evangelii Nuntiandi*, Sacred Congregation for the Doctrine of the Faith.

Rahner, K. (1963), *The Church and the Sacraments*, New York: Herder & Herder.

Ratzinger, J. (1987), *Principles of Catholic Theology*, San Francisco, CA: Ignatius.

Tilby, A. (2008), in S. Croft (ed.), *Mission-shaped Questions*, London: Church House Publishing.

Urwin, L. (2008), in S. Croft (ed.), *Mission-shaped Questions*, London: Church House Publishing.

von Balthasar, H. U. (1995), *Explorations in Theology volume 4*, San Francisco, CA: Ignatius Press.

7

Reflections on Catholic Mission and Social Justice

SIMON MORRIS AND RIC THORPE

SIMON MORRIS

Social Justice and Catholic Church Growth

Involvement in the affairs of the state by bishops has not always been welcome. When in 1926 a group of them sought to be a cause for good in resolving the coal strike by getting employers and unions speaking with each other, Stanley Baldwin, then Prime Minister, wasn't very keen on the idea – he responded to the suggestion by saying he welcomed the intervention as much as he suspected they would have appreciated it if he had asked the Steel and Coal Board to offer a redraft of the Athanasian Creed.

Reflecting on that story, Archbishop William Temple asserts in *Christianity and Social Order* that the Church is to offer principles, not policy, in her interaction with the state. Archbishop Temple cited our Lord's reluctance to be involved in an inheritance dispute as the biblical precedent: 'Friend, who set me to be a judge or arbitrator over you?' The Archbishop's personal suggestions were only published as an appendix to his work.

One of the biggest crises that continues to affect the people of London is the housing shortage and how councils will move people out of London when the third child arrives or whenever their presence becomes inconvenient. This is a direct challenge to the Church's desire to build community and we could have spoken out more about that, not telling the state what policies to adopt, but pointing out what works and what doesn't. We could be clearer, as a Church, about the importance of place. The Church is too often complicit in the malaise in modern culture that being physically in proximity to someone is no longer important. The Church should be part of the fight back against that attitude, or how else can we love our neighbour, the person next to us? We, as Catholics in the Church of England, can show why place is important, a message the nation needs to hear.

A further threat to our building community is the all-pervasive consumerist culture. This too infects the Church. Food banks are providing a great service and many churches are rightly involved in this ministry. But I'm concerned that food banks are the consumerist response to a consumerist-culture problem, and that maybe the Church should be pushing a little harder for people to eat together and not just for folk to take food home to eat there.

The Catechism of the Catholic Church defines social justice as 'respecting the transcendent dignity of man' (section 1929), part of the general virtue of justice, giving to each what is due to them, which of course isn't necessarily the same for everyone. Remember our Lord gives to one person five talents, to another person two, and to yet another just one talent. This will inevitably produce some tension between the world's understanding of social justice and the Church's understanding of it. Fighting euthanasia, for example, is a matter of social justice. Society has a proper concern that women should be given a greater respect and this is something we need to do better in the Church, while not letting society dictate what that looks like. Our ability to contribute to such debates is severely hindered by our not having articulated the foundation issues of what it is to be human before discussing some of the knottier problems.

Society does not have the level of concern that it should for the poor because they really do not have a voice. Yet much of our social justice in our parishes and church institutions will be about the poor. *Gaudium et spes*, the Second Vatican Council's document on the Church in the Modern World, offers the helpful reminder that social justice is not something we as Christians do to others because we are called to be suffering in the same way as others, after the example of Christ (see, for example, sections 22 and 29).

We offer night shelters and lunch clubs and children's work for our own people as well as for the whole community. We do well to remind ourselves and the wider world that our churches will be some of the most diverse places in the country.

But why do we do social justice? I'd like to suggest it's not so that the local council thinks we're relevant, nor because we think the kingdom of God is all about food and drink. Rather, we follow the example of our Lord, who sits and eats with sinners; who washes the feet of the man who is about to deny ever having met him; who heals ten lepers even though he knows only one will come back to thank him. Jesus heals bodies to show he has power and to usher in a kingdom not of this world. And so our social justice is to be subversive as well, speaking about that different kingdom, not being simply – like a post office – an outpost of Her Majesty's Government or a well-intentioned private company.

There are clearly benefits to having good social justice within our parishes: it reaches out to new people, a skill at which generally we're pretty rubbish; it will encourage members of our congregation to realize they can fulfil positions of leadership. But I hope the important thing that putting social justice and church growth together in this conference teaches us is that we do not do the former to achieve the latter. Social justice presumably might even mean we lose a few, just like Jesus lost a few followers when he told them to eat his flesh and drink his blood. The message can be too much for some.

I hope, in fact, that how we do social justice teaches us not to try to measure church growth at all. We cannot tell where the Spirit will blow, or where the seed will sprout roots, and I pray for a day when we stop measuring congregations and how many come to carol services. This will help give the Church the agility it needs in proclaiming the good news of salvation.

RIC THORPE

Finding Common Ground: Social Justice and Church Growth across Traditions

As Bishop of Islington it is a huge honour to contribute to this work and speak into the relationship between church growth and social justice. At first sight, a charismatic evangelical church planter might not have much to say to a conference on Catholic mission, but I have found that there is much common ground that I offer humbly to conversations about mission and social justice.

By way of introduction, I want to share what I have learned from my experience of church planting and revitalization in the East End of London, and also what I have observed in other churches. In 2005, I was invited by the Bishop of London to revitalize the about-to-be-closed St Paul's Shadwell (https:// sps.church/) with a team from Holy Trinity Brompton (HTB) (www.htb.org/).

As soon as we started to research and begin our work in the East End, it was obvious that Anglo-Catholics had gone before us. Many of the great Christian interventions of the past, including stories and methodologies of church planting in the East End of London, had sprung from the Anglo-Catholic mission in the nineteenth century. Through this outreach, people came to faith in Jesus Christ, the poor were reached and supported, churches were built and prospered. I found it a great inspiration to hear these stories and see the impact of this church planting mission on the East End, and they became a huge influence on us at St Paul's Shadwell.

An additional strand in my understanding of social justice came from HTB, where I served for many years. There was a great movement of God's Spirit there in the 1990s, which led to an explosion in evangelism, culminating in the growth of the Alpha Course, which spread across the country and then beyond, touching every tradition globally and involving nearly all denominations of the global Church. At the same time, a social justice movement sprang up, which developed into HTB's ministry to prisoners and ex-offenders, and with the homeless through the work of their night shelter. HTB saw a huge increase in the numbers of volunteers who started working among the poor and marginalized, as well as ministries to older people who were lonely and excluded, and to addicts of all kinds through the recovery courses. This dual strand of evangelism and social justice has greatly influenced my own journey of planting a church – a longing to be evangelistic through proclamation and to come alongside those on the margins in practical ways with the good news of Jesus.

Theology

My incumbent Sandy Millar used to say that for anything we do in the Church, we need a theology, a model and a practice, so that what we do flows out of what we understand of who God is, and what he is doing and wanting to do. First, when exploring the theology of social justice in mission, I am drawn to Jesus' manifesto in Luke 4, alluding to Isaiah 61. The first words that Jesus speaks in public when he reads aloud in the synagogue are these:

> The Spirit of the Lord is upon me,
>   because he has anointed me to bring good news to
>   the poor.

He has sent me to proclaim release to the captives
  and recovery of sight to the blind,
  to let the oppressed go free,
to proclaim the year of the Lord's favour. (Luke 4.18–19)

Jesus then sat down and said, 'Today this scripture has been fulfilled in your hearing' (Luke 4.21). Imagine being in the synagogue and hearing these words – it is an extraordinary moment! Jesus chose these words to show that his mission was anointed by the Holy Spirit. It was a mission to the poor and broken-hearted, to those in prison, captive to addictions and in mourning. And he announces it with his followers in mind. When he said 'Follow me' to the disciples, he was inviting them into this mission too. As one person said, it is a mission to the last, the lost and the least. These words also remind me of Isaiah 58, where God said to the people of Israel:

If you remove the yoke from among you,
  the pointing of the finger, the speaking of evil,
if you offer your food to the hungry
  and satisfy the needs of the afflicted,
then your light shall rise in the darkness
  and your gloom be like the noonday.
The LORD will guide you continually,
  and satisfy your needs in parched places,
  and make your bones strong;
and you shall be like a watered garden,
  like a spring of water,
  whose waters never fail.
Your ancient ruins shall be rebuilt;
  you shall raise up the foundations of many generations;
you shall be called the repairer of the breach,
  the restorer of streets to live in. (Isa. 58.9–12)

This is again a call to the poor, the marginalized and the oppressed, which is empowered and anointed by the Holy Spirit. Together these passages have become the theological foundation of my thinking on this subject.

Alongside these Scriptures, we might consider a theology of place. As Anglican priests and incumbents, we are given the cure of souls so that every person in every parish is prayed for and considered in some way with the mission of Christ. There are many ways this can impact our theological thinking, but one way is by walking our streets, meeting the people of our parishes, and prayerfully discerning their realities and needs. As we pray these Scriptures on our streets, we cannot but help ask this question: what does this look like here?

Models

So what might this look like today? What models are there to base this work on? In practice, among the many ways this can be done, I have seen this operate in two dimensions – with 'who' is involved and 'where' it is focused.

The 'who' can involve something more corporate that a particular local church as a whole chooses to focus on. This might be something that the local church invests money, time and energy in by praying and discerning the needs around them. For example, if there are many people struggling with debt both in our congregation and the community around them, we could explore a Christians Against Poverty initiative. This activates social justice in the life of the Church, becoming visible and tangible and something that members can join in with and support. It's often helpful to focus on one or two areas, instead of championing every need as we might not have the resources to support them properly. This might be the way that a local church responds to a local injustice or social need.

The 'who' can also involve individuals who are passionate about a particular social justice cause or project. They might draw others from the church into this work, but it is not necessarily given much airtime in the local church. It might be that many people are involved as individuals, in the myriad opportunities and possibilities around them, whether local or global. In our congregations, we might encourage each person to be involved in some kind of social justice by simply asking, 'How are you responding to the poor?' It could be encouraging people to buy a homeless person a cup of coffee or engaging personally with those who are hurting and broken and allowing them to change us.

The other dimension is 'where' this mission and ministry is focused. There are some social justice missions that the church can host or organize using its own facilities, like using the church nave, a church hall, or members' homes. This is, in essence, something that the local church is responsible for. If it wasn't hosted by the local church, it would not happen.

The other 'where' is somewhere else, not hosted by the local church or by church members, but hosted by someone or something else. It is organized and hosted elsewhere and is supported by the church or by members of the church.

Whatever dimension is being considered, whether corporate or individual, or inside or outside the Church, this focus is kindled as the Church answers the question of how we respond to the needs of those around us. How can we love our neighbour? And, as leaders, we can bless and encourage these different approaches.

Practices

Once we have a grasp of the theology involved – why we are doing this, and some ideas of models (how we might do this) – we can see what is being done in practice. I want to do this by exploring three different stories involving church plants and revitalizations that I have seen or been directly involved with on the ground.

In 2009, a group of 30 people moved from HTB to Brighton. They were invited by the Bishop of Chichester to restart a church in Brighton called St Peter's (https://stpeters-brighton.org/). The team relocated and St Peter's began to grow, as they ran Alpha courses and intentionally reached out to their neighbours. At the same time, as the team prayed together, God touched their hearts about the homeless. It's a major problem in Brighton and they felt God calling them to start a homeless shelter and ministry to the homeless. This ministry has become a key part of life at St Peter's, involving 385 volunteer members. There are people serving in the night shelter who are trained and have a lot of experience working with the homeless. But St Peter's have also made it possible for normal members of the church to be involved in simple ways. It has helped their congregation feel empowered to be part of this ministry and many people are now involved. There have been several spin-offs, such as the Safehaven Women ministry, which gives vulnerable women the chance to meet together and relax in a safe environment with homemade meals, a clothes bank, crafts and hairdressing.

More recently, in 2014, St Swithun's Church in Bournemouth was reopened when a team of ten people, led by the Revd Tim Matthews, relocated from London at the invitation of the Bishop of Winchester. The church grew very quickly, and as they prayed around the area they asked God, 'What are you calling us to do in this place?' They started to find syringes and needles in the churchyard, and they realized that the churchyard had become a place where people were taking drugs. God broke their hearts for these people, and they started a recovery course. Now the council regards this as one of the most successful rehabilitation programmes for addicts in the borough. When they sent their first church planting team to revitalize St Clement's Boscombe, again at the invitation of the bishop, it soon became clear that the community there had even greater addiction issues. The new community at St Clement's can now support recovery courses and programmes there too, drawing on the experience and support of St Swithun's Bournemouth.

A third example is from Shadwell, where I spent 11 years. We had a group of middle-class people in our congregation who worked in finance, yet we were surrounded by significant urban poverty. One of them, who worked with KPMG and served as treasurer on the PCC, started a debt advice service, meeting people to help them with their finances. They then began getting referrals from local agencies and GP practices, and started to support clients through court proceedings and renegotiating debt. It was powerful to watch how something changed in the hearts of the people providing this ministry: initially they were doing it for the poor, but God began to change their hearts as they prayed and met with their clients. They began to receive as much, if not more, from the people they were encountering. Some have become friends and some have joined the church. 'For' the poor has become 'with' the poor.

As I've worked with church planting teams all around the country, I have seen this pattern repeat itself again and again. Initially, a planting or revitalizing team starts in a new area where everything is new – they are unknown and do not know what is happening locally. Yet, as the incarnational work grows, as the gospel impacts those around them, God transforms the church members' hearts and deepens their love for their community. As we recognize that the Spirit of God is the one who calls us and anoints us to bring good news to the poor, we are changed more and more into God's likeness, becoming a catalyst for God's kingdom.

In my experience of this growing movement of church planting and revitalization, I am seeing more and more that there is no separation between evangelism and social justice. Both are at the forefront of its mission. The very DNA of this movement includes compassion for the poor, the broken, the captives and the prisoners. And that is affecting the membership of these growing churches, as the last, the least and the lost come to faith and find a place and a home in these churches. It is also affecting the places this movement is going to as they plant, not just in city centres but also in the harder to reach estates and people groups.

As a final word, I believe that God is calling us to work together more, across former divisions of tradition and practice. We have so much to learn from one another. I myself have learned so much from the Anglo-Catholic mission in the East End, and that has had a huge influence on my thinking and practice. However, I have so much more to learn. And it is the whole Church, in all its traditions and tribes, that God calls to love and transform his world.

Bibliography

Chapman, Geoffrey (1994), *Catechism of the Catholic Church*, Vatican City: Libreria Editrice Vaticana.

'Gaudium et Spes', in Norman P. Tanner (ed.) (1990), *Decrees of the Ecumenical Councils*, volume 2, New York: Sheed & Ward.

Holy Trinity Brompton, www.htb.org/.

St Paul's Shadwell, https://sps.church/.

St Peter's Church Brighton, https://stpetersbrighton.org/.

St Swithun's Bournemouth: www.lovechurch.org/

PART 3

Reflections on Scripture

8

A Sermon at Evensong at the End of the First Day of the Anglican Catholic Future / Forward in Faith Conference 18 September 2018

ANNA MATTHEWS

Exodus 16.1–12
Mark 8.1–10, 14–20

It is six weeks since the waters had parted and the people had seen God act to fulfil his promise of deliverance, but memories are already fading. Miriam's song, sung in jubilant, incredulous praise from the far side of the sea, already seems to belong to a different era. Now is the time of doubt – of aching feet and rumbling bellies, of fear for the future – that crowds out remembrance of the past. Caught up in the drama of the Passover night, their midnight escape with nothing but their kneading bowls on their backs had seemed a bold act of faith. In the harsh light of the desert, trust in God seems merely foolish.

Tired and hungry in this endless and inhospitable wilderness, the people turn to nostalgia and to grumbling. It was better in Egypt. If only we could put the clock back. Our leaders have led us astray, are taking us in the wrong direction, don't know what they're doing. This is not what we thought obeying God would mean. Where's the promised land with its rivers of milk and honey? We're better off turning back, returning to the familiar. We must save ourselves.

It would be quite wrong to draw too many parallels between the Israelites in the wilderness and Catholics in the Church of England. But I suspect (I hope!) I am not the only one who finds herself prey to the twin dangers of nostalgia and grumbling. It happens when I feel insecure, when I find myself in a place that feels odd or unfamiliar, when I'm driven by a fear of scarcity, of not having enough, or not being enough.

Nostalgia, in such circumstances, offers an escape from the present. Whether you want to turn the clock back to pre-1992 or pre-Second Vatican Council, or whether you think the flesh-pots of 'the good old days' lie in the Oxford Movement or the medieval Church, nostalgia is an attitude that looks back-wards. The Promised Land is behind you. And when you're busy looking behind you all the time, or seeking to re-create those days in the present, you risk missing what God's up to now.

But that mustn't mean discounting the past. Israel, through-out its history, is commanded to recount the gracious deeds of the Lord. Remembering, particularly liturgical remembering, is what helps Israel to be Israel. It's what helps them attend to the thread of promise woven through their history of exodus and exile: the consistent story of God's faithfulness. In fact, it's forgetfulness of history that so often leads them into idolatry and disaster. When they forget the past, they forget who they are and who God is. True remembering, the lively inhabiting of tradition, is a counter to nostalgia, because it encourages trust. When we remember what God has done for us, corporately and individually, we remember that God is faithful. And that helps us to look to the future with hope rather than fear. And we have such rich treasures to share to help us in this: Scrip-tures and sacraments that draw us into the story of salvation, that name us and claim us as Christ's own; rites and traditions that help us to see the world anew, now that in Christ flesh and bread and water and oil and touch are made bearers of God's grace. Those of us called as stewards of the holy mysteries need to be expansive in sharing them, confident that even when others have become forgetful or can't see their point, these are the places of God's abiding faithfulness, and the Church can't be the Church without them.

So for the sake of the Church and of the world, we need to be people who sing, with Miriam, of the Lord who has triumphed gloriously; and sing with Mary of the God who fills the hungry soul with good. These are songs that form us as a people of thankful remembering and expectant hope.

This sort of remembering is also a good antidote to grumbling, because it's a provocation to gratitude, to Eucharistic living. For the Israelites in the wilderness, it's fear of scarcity that makes them grumble – about the conditions, about Moses, about what they think God ought to be doing. They grumble in a way that corrodes community and trust. And I all too easily catch myself joining in with those grumbling Israelites, picking holes in the latest diocesan strategy or initiative, bemoaning the focus on Fresh Expressions at the expense of the parish, alarmed by everything that's being poured into big resource churches while everyone else is left fighting over crumbs.

Grumbling comes about as a result of the fear of scarcity: there isn't enough. Whether it's bread, or money, or time, or resources, fear of scarcity tells you that you'd better secure your own future, at someone else's expense if need be. Remembering the goodness of God, however, giving thanks for all he has done, helps shape our imagination and expectation of all he is doing and will do. It helps us find manna in the wilderness.

In the wilderness, the Israelites had to learn to trust God to provide. And God did. His provision didn't look like what they expected: this odd, flaky stuff that melts in the heat of the day and rots when they try to hoard it. He gives them their daily bread, reminding them that they are sustained not by their own efforts but by his generosity, and that he is enough.

It's a similar story in the New Testament reading. The disciples, slow as ever in St Mark's Gospel, are fixated on the one loaf of bread they've brought with them, fretting that there won't be enough, and that they'll go hungry. Already they're forgetful of the multiplications, of the basketsful left over, of the bread of abundance. And so, instead of recognizing the Bread of Life right there in the boat with them, they worry over the loaf. Jesus can feed them with the inexhaustible plenitude of God, but they will argue over how to divide up the loaf, and bicker over who gets the crumbs.

The Church is contained in that boat. And often, like the disciples, we still don't understand; we think we have no bread. We think we have to rely on our own resources. We pay lip service to God but make plans and strategies based on our fear that he won't come through on his promises. We argue over the loaf of scarcity and forget that Jesus is in the boat with us.

In a Church and a world where fear of scarcity often drives things, the Catholic witness does not need to be to fight for a bigger slice of the loaf of scarcity. It is, instead, to recognize the gift of our hunger for the living bread, and through this to live with faith in God's abundance: to help people recognize the bread that comes down from heaven to give life to the world, to open up the space for people to know and love Jesus Christ.

There is, it strikes me, often a sense of anxiety around when Catholics talk about mission, as though it's a strange new art we need to learn. And there are good things for us to learn from the wider Church. But we already know what to do, and we've been given what we need. We don't need to save ourselves: God has already done that. If we really believe that the Church continues the ministry of Jesus Christ, then our mission is to be like him: for our churches to be places, communities, that speak and act and love like him. To those whose lives are dominated by scarcity he offers shelter, community and sustenance in night shelters and refuges, in food banks and credit unions, and in the gathered, motley people of God. To the burdened, the lost and the broken he offers freedom and forgiveness; and to every hungry soul he gives himself as true food, the gift that is the source and summit of all our mission.

In the wilderness God provides manna to an anxious, grumbling people whose faith had faltered. And there they learn that they need not be afraid; that they are sustained by his faithfulness and generosity. On the shores of the Sea of Galilee and in the desert, thousands saw Jesus take a small offering of bread and fish and feed a multitude. And from this we can take courage that when we offer our own gifts, even when we're fearful that they're not enough, that we're not enough, God is always enough: the God who is faithful takes and blesses and breaks and gives us and our offerings and makes them the vehicle for his abundance.

9

'With God there is no Zero-Sum': A Sermon for the Closing Mass of the Anglican Catholic Future / Forward in Faith Conference 20 September 2018

ANDREW DAVISON

Isaiah 60.1–6
John 17.6–25

'Arise, shine, for your light has come.' We find so much of what makes us rejoice to be Anglo-Catholics in our first reading, from Isaiah. At the centre is Isaiah's promise that salvation gathers us into a community. Then, in God's word of hope coming to people whose lives are dark, we recognize our pastoral and parochial heritage. And right through, there's the promise of light. There's glory in abundance. At the end, there's even incense.

Across these past two days, we've heard a good deal about God's abundance. And now I myself want to point to the generosity of God, in two unlikely words: in two of John's prepositions, 'through' and 'to'. I'll come to that in a moment.

Christians should be wary of the 'zero-sum game'. We should beware an assumption that more of *this* implies *less* of that; be wary of any suggestion that competition rules the day.

A Catholic vision denies that. You don't need *less* of the

Church to have more of the kingdom; you don't need *less* sacrament to have more word; we need not have *less* that's material to have more that's spiritual, or *less* of Mary to have more of Jesus. With Christ before us, we see that you don't need to have *less* of humanity to have more of God.

In our Gospel, Jesus talks about 'those who will believe in me *through* their word': through *our* words. There's no zero-sum there: it's not God's word *or* ours; it's God's word *through* ours. It's not less of what is human, so that there can be more of what's divine.

A few lines later, in verse 22, Jesus says to the Father, 'The glory that you have given me *I have given them*.' Let's not underestimate that *giving to*. Glory among God's children doesn't diminish the glory of God; it manifests it. And God does not shine *for us*; God *makes us* shine.

This is a Catholic vision: not less of the Church so there can be more of God; not less of human action so there can be more of God's; not less of glory among women and men so there can be more of the glory of God; not less human in order to be more divine.

All of this reminds me of a wonderful phrase from one of Alison Milbank's books: that God makes things not 'transparent but rather radiant' (Milbank, 2009, p. 25). Not transparent – transparency is generic – but radiant: radiant in its distinct way. God doesn't rub out the particularity of things to communicate through them. Rather, God makes things – makes us – more perfectly what we are, to be radiant with God's glory. Are St Dominic or St Clare transparent? Better, instead, to say that Dominic is radiant, in his distinct way, and Clare in hers.

'Not transparent but radiant' – the phrase beautifully embodies the no-zero-sum point. We are not effaced to make God more present, or more active. 'The glory you have given me I *have given them*'; others will come to believe '*through* their word'.

This conference was a risk. We threw our bread upon the waters, to see what comes of it. It has already returned to us bountifully. We close with a Mass for the Evangelization of Peoples; for me – and I am sure for many of you – it is also a Mass of Thanksgiving for what we have shared.

This conference embodies the theological principles I've mentioned. Within the grace of God, there is no zero-sum. For one perspective to flourish more, another does not need to flourish less. The well-being of one group of us does not require less well-being of another. The glory of God is not better manifest if we are all effaced, rubbed out, made the same: better to be radiant in our distinct ways, than generically transparent.

Naturally enough, we've concentrated on what's distinctive about our tradition. Obviously so. Let's pray that these days have fostered confidence in that, in our Anglo-Catholic witness. But for all I want to press the Anglo-Catholic case, I'm reminded that there's no zero-sum within the grace of God; God's abundance does away with the need for competition.

For me, that suggests we should rejoice in what we have, but not want to hoard it; that we should rejoice in what we have, and be grateful for what others also have: grateful for what they already share with us, and for what is distinctly their own. Nothing about our life as Anglo-Catholics, about our witness, or our tradition, is diminished for also being found among other Christians; nor will we become less by sharing what we have. We have nothing that we did not receive, nothing that was not meant to be shared.

I don't know what our next step should be, but I hope we will continue to walk more closely together, for the sake of the Church and the world: entering further into the promise, in our Gospel, 'that they may be one, as we are one'.

I hope that – made confident by the abundance of God – one next step will be to find ways to talk about the treasures we share: to talk not only among ourselves, but also with the wider Church.

Not everyone will want to draw from our wells, but many will. A Church with so *few* theological and ecclesiological bearings can be newly open to Catholic ones. The pragmatic mood in our Church can be disheartening, but it may also leave it open to learning from our tradition, when it does so many things so obviously well. And, as the other side of this, a truly confident Anglo-Catholicism wouldn't find learning from others a diminishment, but a gain.

'Arise, shine, for your light has come.' This message takes us beyond scarcity. Others will come to believe *through* our words. Truly, the glory of God is *given to us*: indeed, as we kneel in a moment, the glory of God will be given into our hands.

Bibliography

Milbank, Alison (2009), *Chesterton and Tolkien as Theologians: The Fantasy of the Real*, London: T & T Clark.

PART 4

Catholic Mission in Historical Perspective

10

Catholic Mission within Anglicanism – Identifying Core Principles

STEPHEN SPENCER

Where to start? This is always a vexed question for Catholic-minded Anglicans. The modern Catholic Revival began in the nineteenth century with the assertion that the Church of England was part of the one holy catholic and apostolic Church with its faith and order rooted in the undivided Church of the first four centuries and with its connection to all this expressed through the apostolic succession of the episcopacy. To undertake an overview of Catholic mission would therefore require beginning with the growth and spread of the Church in those early centuries, continuing through the rise and splitting of Christendom in the medieval and Reformation eras, and only at the end surveying developments within the Church of England and the Anglican Communion in the last two centuries.

However, this book is being produced for a specific context and moment in time: for adherents of the Catholic Revival within Anglicanism that derives from the Oxford Movement of 1833 to 1845, and from the movement of renewal that sprung from that – variously known as Tractarianism, Puseyism, Ritualism, Anglo-Catholicism or simply Catholicism. This movement has suffered from recent sharp division over the ordination of women, but this book is being produced with the purpose of recovering what is common to both sides of that split so that a new phase of renewal and growth may be launched. This chapter contributes to that common endeavour by focusing on how early adherents of the movement have engaged in mission and, specifically, on uncovering the key principles of that engagement, so that those principles may be expressed in fresh and creative ways in a renewed Catholic mission for today.

I

With those terms of reference in mind, it is therefore appropriate to begin this survey in Oxford in 1833 with John Keble's sermon in the university church before the Assize judges. This sermon is widely regarded as launching the Oxford Movement, and with it a surge of renewal that grew and spread through Anglicanism in the nineteenth and early twentieth centuries. Yet the oddness of beginning here is that Keble's sermon was anything but an attempt to launch a mission movement. It was, in fact, an attempt to resist challenges from the state to the Church's authority and status. Keble accused the Whig government of committing no less than apostasy by seeking to abolish a number of Anglican bishoprics in Ireland. How could a government that included nonconformists, Roman Catholics and even atheists have the right to interfere in the Church of England's faith and order? So Keble's sermon was, on the face of it, an essentially reactive and conservative response to the changing political and economic landscape of 1830s Britain. Here was a deeply respected priest of a church that previously had benefited from the privileges and power of being the religious arm of the state now protesting when some of the connections between the two were being severed.

Yet in a remarkable paradox this conservatism became the seedbed of a huge movement of change. Keble came from the heartlands of Tory England; he embodied the longstanding marriage of the Church of England with the monarchy, aristocracy, landed gentry and settled ways of life in the rural shires, a way of life in which everyone had a place and value. But now he was raising his voice in protest against the current custodians of that order, the government in Westminster. If a radical had made accusations against the government it is likely that no one would have taken much notice, but the fact that it was Keble accusing the government made the assembled congregation – and, shortly afterwards, other members of senior common rooms across Oxford – react with a mixture of shock and wonder. Clearly, even in Oxford, the political situation was now very serious and something had to be done to protect the Church. This was precisely the reaction of a group of young Anglican clergy led by the vicar of the university church, John Henry Newman, who decided that a campaign must be launched. This group believed the clergy of the Church of England must be recruited and equipped to resist the state's attacks upon its faith and order. So, in order to shore up their learning and resolve, the group would write, publish and distribute a series of 'Tracts for the Times'. They would employ the new postal system to send freshly written pamphlets to rectories and vicarages up and down the land. They would present a range of theological and ecclesiological arguments to rouse the clergy from an outlook that allowed a wide latitude of belief and practice, and show how there were deep and robust reasons why the orthodox faith and practice of the Church must be defended. Newman's *Tract 1* epitomizes this rallying purposiveness by drawing its readers back to the foundation of the Church's authority:

CHRIST has not left His Church without claim of its own upon the attention of men. Surely not. Hard Master He cannot be, to bid us oppose the world, yet give us no credentials for so doing. I fear we have neglected the real ground on which our authority is built,—our APOSTOLICAL DESCENT.

We have been born, not of blood, nor of the will of the flesh, nor of the will of man, but of GOD. The LORD JESUS CHRIST gave His SPIRIT to His Apostles; they in turn laid their hands on those who should succeed them; and these again on others; and so the sacred gift has been handed down to our present Bishops, who have appointed us as their assistants, and in some sense representatives. (Newman, 1833)

Here, then, Newman was presenting a powerful case for the Church of England to acknowledge and live out its own inherent authority vis-à-vis the state. Whereas up to this point many clergy had assumed that the authority of the Church derived from its establishment with the state, and especially from the monarch as Supreme Governor of the Church, now Newman was showing that the Church had an authority that was independent of all this. It was, in fact, an authority much more ancient than that of the British monarchy and was tangibly visible in the solemn rites of episcopal consecrations and ordinations. Christ, no less, was present and active in the Church and would empower it for what lay ahead.

After a period in which conservative churchmen had felt beleaguered by the reforming pressures of the state, here was a shift in mindset that would give them confidence in the institution they served and would make them want to renew, promote and extend its life wherever possible. Here was the source of energy and inspiration that Newman's readership, and the undergraduates who heard him preach week by week in the university church and would later be ordained into the ministry of that church, would take out to the parishes and, later on, to the establishing of new churches in the growing urban and industrial areas of the country. A first principle of Catholic mission, then, could be summarized in the following way: that it is born and given energy by sharp anger and protest at the secularizing pressures of modern society, pressures that have cut people off from their connectedness with God and his

Church, and that this protest finds expression in a determination to regain awareness and confidence in Christ's presence in the Church, a presence tangibly handed down through apostolic succession.

A good example of this, one that became a kind of paradigm for the movement as a whole, was Keble's ministry in his rural parish in Hampshire. In many ways this was a deeply conventional ministry, with Keble taking services in the parish church according to the Book of Common Prayer without any of the ritualism that would later become associated with the movement, and with diligent pastoral care of his parishioners. But the rationale for doing this was not based on habit and convention but because it was through the life of a parish church within a parochial community that a Catholic identity and holiness would truly be formed: 'The unit of the parish was the means by which organic pre-commercial society and its concomitant social harmony might be reclaimed ... a conscious repudiation of statist or societal solutions' (Skinner, 2004, p. 144). The vision was of recovering a Catholic way of life holistically encompassing Church and community, one that was perceived as existing before the Reformation and the more recent ravages of the Industrial Revolution, and that was in opposition to the dislocating and alienating pressures of these movements.

The integrity of what Keble was about is shown in his committed and self-sacrificial pastoral ministry. He knew the problems of poverty, the difficulties of the domestic economy, the ravages of disease. His writings show him 'commenting on farm labourers breaking machines, the conditions of workhouses, beer-houses and their effects on the population, the price of corn and the distribution of allotments' (Skinner, 2004, pp. 145–6). He was frequently ill from his visitations to the parish sick. He was proactive in practical and astute ways, such as sponsoring the creation of allotments for those without land, founding a parish savings bank in the hope of encouraging poor parishioners to save during seasonally high wages, and, if all else failed, supporting emigration schemes (Skinner, 2004, p. 146).

This ministry led Keble in some radical directions, then, a long way from his quiescent upbringing. It again illustrates the paradox of Catholic mission, that while it arose out of reaction to social and political change it became a movement of progressive change for local churches and communities. It also suggests that a second principle of Catholic mission might be that its paradigmatic expression is through a self-sacrificial ministry with those in need, one that does not just respond to immediate need but takes a proactive approach to addressing causes of poverty.

II

What kind of theology underpinned the nascent Oxford Movement? One of the clearest expressions came from the second generation of leaders, and in particular Robert Isaac Wilberforce. He was the son of the great evangelical reformer William Wilberforce but, like his brother Samuel, moved away from the evangelicalism of his father and became a committed follower of the Tractarians. He rose through the hierarchy of the Church to become Archdeacon of the East Riding of York-shire. Addressing the clergy in his archdeaconry in 1846, he began by describing the type of organic mission that Keble so powerfully embodied:

the Church of Christ is the real bond of national life, the true principle of concord among men, the redresser of the fall, the assertion of a federal being and family alliance, whereby all members of Christ are made members of one another. (Wilberforce, 1846, p. 14)

Wilberforce then highlighted the importance of the incarnation to this vision of the Church at the heart of society: if only churchmen could realize 'the marvellous fact of his Incarnation, that crowning mystery, whereby GODHEAD and Manhood, whereby matter and spirit are indissolubly combined', then they might truly understand 'their birth-right' as 'members of the Christian family'. The Church, then, had its own authority rooted in Christ's incarnation, an authority over every member of society quite distinct from the authority of the state. Wilberforce wanted church people to truly absorb this theology into their whole way of thinking: 'Such a habit would re-act upon their belief, as well as upon their worship; they would understand better the purposes for which they met, and the nature of that society which held them together' (Skinner, 2004, pp. 259–60).

Two years later Wilberforce published one of the most significant theological texts of the movement, *The Doctrine of the Incarnation of Our Lord Jesus Christ in its Relation to Mankind and the Church* (1848). In the conclusion of the book, as he drew the threads of his argument together, he described how the doctrine of the incarnation had profound implications for the status of rich and poor in society, implications that the Church must express: it 'must preach humility in the palace and self-respect in the lowly hovels of the poor. It must enforce such lessons of self-denial as may mitigate the glare of earthly splendour, while it compensates the afflicted for the necessary privations of their lot' (Wilberforce, 1848, p. 547).

Catholic mission, then, was ultimately about bringing every member of society into the Church, a society of equals in which the rich kneel alongside the poor in the family of Christ, by the one who has authority to bring this about because of the incarnation, the mystery of divinity and humanity united in his own person. A third principle of Catholic mission is therefore something like this: that it is not only about ministry to those in need but also, ultimately, about the incorporation of all people into the society of the Church, a society of equals with divine authority deriving from God incarnate, the one who unites divinity and humanity in his own person.

While Wilberforce did not remain in the Church of England, following Newman into the Roman Catholic Church in 1854, his theology found increasingly elaborate expression in the ministry of a number of pioneering parishes in poor areas. One of the most famous is St Alban's in Holborn, London. It was opened in 1862 in an area of great deprivation to the north of the City of London. Conditions in the poor districts of London were desperate, with squalor, disease and often starvation being common. One priest wrote of 'the murky atmosphere of fog and dust' pervading the narrow courts and alleys, with half-naked children playing in the gutter, 'many of them stunted, half-witted and deformed, and all wan and sickly looking' (Rowell, 1983, p. 117). Alexander Mackonochie was the vicar of St Alban's from 1862 to 1882 and, to the wonder of many outside observers, he made it very clear that the church was for everyone and especially for the poor. There would be no pews reserved for those who could afford to pay rents for their use. Slowly but surely he encouraged the poor to come into the church and make it their own: 'The bonnetless and the shoeless were in sufficient numbers, and as there were no pew-rents and no appropriations, they were enabled to feel that they had as good a right to their own church as anyone else' (M. Reynolds in Hylson-Smith, 1998, p. 70).

To encourage different age groups to belong to the church Mackonochie developed guilds and associations for men and boys, and for women and girls, and various other agencies ranging from a blanket-loan fund to a cricket club. The results were dramatic: 'From the time of its consecration until 1867 there was steady progress, with large and increasing congregations. The annual total number of communicants rose from about 3,000 to more than 18,000' (Hylson-Smith, 1998, p. 71).

What, though, was the nature of the religion that these poor parishioners would find within these new churches? St Alban's was an early example of a type of church that appeared across many of the industrial cities of Britain. Another and slightly earlier example was the Church of St Barnabas, Pimlico, under

William Bennett. This church was founded out of the smart parish church of St Paul's, Knightsbridge, in 1846–7, to serve the poor of the parish. Bennett was a devoted pastor as well as being one of the leaders of the Tractarian Movement. He knew that preaching theological principles from the pulpit would not be enough: there was a need for some visual and kinaesthetic representation of the theology of the movement, and especially of the central place of the sacraments in mission. He looked to the ritual of the medieval Catholic Church to do this. Thus he placed two lighted candles on the altar, to indicate the presence of the light of Christ at the table, and faced east for the prayer of consecration, east being the direction from which Christ would return in glory. This was in contrast to standing at the north side of the table, as stipulated in the rubrics at the start of the Lord's Supper in the Book of Common Prayer. Furthermore, he allowed some of the communicants to receive the bread directly into their mouths, so that they did not finger the bread that was increasingly being seen as itself the body of Christ; nor did he hand over the chalice to the communicant during Communion but, to show greater reverence for the blood of Christ, took it to their lips himself. He also began his sermons with the refrain, 'In the name of the Father and of the Son and of the Holy Ghost', and used the sign of the cross. These were medieval Catholic practices and were also found in the contemporary Roman Catholic Church, whose hierarchy had recently been legalized and revived with a great flourish in Britain (having attracted high-profile converts such as Newman and Wilberforce, as we have seen). Another principle of Catholic mission would therefore be this: that it finds engaging ways of communicating with the people it is seeking to reach using multi-sensory forms of sacramental worship that enrich and supplement the written and spoken word.

But this would result in trouble for Bennett, for where he saw ancient Catholicism others saw 'popery' (a selling-out of English religion to the foreign Pope of Rome). The Bishop of London, Charles Blomfield, objected to Bennett's innovations and sought to get them stopped. The case was reported in the press and soon St Barnabas' was swamped with supporters and angry opponents who accused Bennett of popery. The opponents threatened to pull the church down and the police were called to keep order. Bennett was eventually forced to resign by Blomfield, and moved to a parish in Frome in Somerset (Chadwick, 1971, pp. 301–3).

But the controversy showed that the adherents of 'ritualism' were profoundly committed to the radical type of mission that it represented, and other clergy decided to support it. In 1857 one of the assistant clergy at St Barnabas', Charles Lowder (1820–80), moved to a mission-house in the very poor East London parish of St George's-in-the-East. He moved with a fraternity of other priests calling themselves the Society of the Holy Cross, and they created a kind of religious community in the mission-house (following a pattern of living together that the clergy at St Saviour's in Leeds had pioneered). They organized daily prayer, frequent preaching, a boys' choir and Bible instruction classes. They constructed an iron church in the garden of the house where they started to wear vestments for the celebration of communion (rather than normal cassock and surplice), again following medieval and current Roman practice. As in Pimlico, fierce opposition developed, mainly from people outside the parish, who stirred up crowds from within the parish to disrupt the services. In 1859 worship was disturbed for months by shouting, whistling, the letting off of firecrackers, and vandalism to church furnishings. But Lowder was 'a brave withdrawn man with a steely will' (Chadwick, 1971, p. 498). He was not to be deterred and noted, 'The very dregs of the people were taught to think about religion. Many were brought to church through the unhappy notoriety ... and some who came to scoff remained to worship' (Rowell, 1983, p. 131).

These riots were reported in the national press, and the National Protestant Society and the 'Anti-Puseyite League' sponsored some of the protesters. None the less, Lowder and his fellow-workers persisted in their labours, and the work moved forward. Public interest and sympathy were aroused by the evident dedication of the fraternity, and in particular by the devoted service of Lowder and his staff during the East London cholera epidemic of 1856. By the time of his death in 1880, Lowder had won the affection and respect of the East End population whom he had lovingly served for almost 40 years. He had gained the honourable title of Father Lowder (Hylson-Smith, 1998, pp. 69–70). Catholic mission, then, is not daunted by opposition but actually grows and strengthens through it. Another principle lies here, then: that Catholic mission is strengthened by the dialectic of conflict with those who would repress it.

Bennett, Mackonochie, Lowder and their churches express a centripetal form of mission, in which people are drawn into the worship of the Church, with ritualism in Eucharistic worship as central, because it 'embodied as nothing else could the sense of the reality of Divine grace in a way which could be grasped by the poor and unlettered' (Rowell, 1983, p. 117). Lowder 'considered that it was as much his duty as a parish priest to put before the eyes of his people the pattern of the worship in Heaven, as it was his duty to preach the Gospel' (Rowell, 1983, p. 133).

Mackonochie also promoted this tradition of using Catholic ritual in worship, which again generated violent and persistent protest from parties outside the parish, including legal action sponsored by the Church Association. This Protestant body spent £40,000 in legal action between 1868 and 1880, and scores of priests were prosecuted. The association objected most strongly to the doctrine of the real presence of Christ in the Eucharist, and tried to ban the elevation of the bread and the wine during the Eucharistic prayer (which symbolized this doctrine), as well as excessive kneeling during the prayer of consecration, ceremonial use of incense, adding water to the wine in the chalice (another medieval practice) and altar lights. 'The Church Association hounded Mackonochie for year after year, but in the end the ritualism was not stopped, little was achieved, though Mackonochie himself was a broken man. He died on holiday, in the snow at night on a bare mountain in Scotland, guarded only by his two dogs' (Hylson-Smith, 1998, p. 72). His funeral, like that of Lowder, drew vast and silent crowds who demonstrated a deep and lasting respect for this pioneer of Catholic renewal. Conflict had its costs, and these should not be underestimated. The principle of engaging in the dialectic of conflict was also, then, a costly engagement.

For the Catholic movement as a whole, sacramental worship was therefore to be at the heart of mission, for this was where unity with Christ was given physical and spiritual expression. This worship was to be in a Christian fellowship that did not derive its legitimacy from establishment with the state, but had its own inherent authority that came through the apostolic succession from Christ himself. It was a fellowship for all people and not just the wealthy, which meant it was specially welcoming to the poor and marginalized in society. It was a worship that would take place in buildings ordered and decorated for this purpose, with a focus upon font and altar rather than lectern and pulpit (though these still had a part to play). The worship was to be ordered with a form of ritual that would draw attention to the real presence of Christ within the sacrament. This would, in turn, transform church buildings from preaching boxes to holy temples, where Christ, the holy of holies, would be present at the altar, uniting earth and heaven.

III

But was the leadership of Catholic mission only for priests operating out of their parish churches? The revival of the religious life shows this not to be the case. The revival began with Pusey in 1839 who suggested that committed women might join a 'sisters of charity', who would 'begin by regular employment as nurses, in hospitals and lunatic asylums, in which

Christian nursing is so sadly missed' (Rowell, 1983, p. 93). In this Pusey was influenced by French seventeenth-century religious communities, such as the sisters of St Vincent de Paul, who combined a monastic lifestyle with service to the poor. Dr Hook, the vicar of Leeds, was supportive of the idea and had a sister who was drawn to such a life, but he warned that this type of development might arouse suspicion from those who opposed anything resembling a Catholic religious order. Pusey, though, was not to be deflected. In 1841 he enabled Marian Rebecca Hughes to become the first person to make a religious profession in the modern Church of England. She made her profession in Oxford in front of Pusey and then attended a communion service celebrated by Newman at the university church. It would take a few years before a community was formed around her, but in 1849 she became the first Superior of the Convent of the Holy and Undivided Trinity at Oxford. Meanwhile, in 1845 Pusey had founded another female religious community at Park Village, Regents Park in London. These sisters were to visit the poor or the sick in their own homes, visit hospitals, workhouses, or prisons, instruct destitute children, and assist in the burial of the dead. By 1850 they had established a daily pattern of saying the monastic services (the offices) interspersed with their work commitments. One novice reported the pattern in the following way, showing a deeply committed form of Catholic mission both new and ancient:

The sisters rose at five ... The service called Lauds was at six a.m., said in the Oratory ... at a quarter to seven the Sisters assembled in the same room and Prime was said ... Breakfast followed, which was taken in silence; indeed silence was observed all day, except at the hours appointed for recreation. After the meal we said Terce and then went to hear Morning Prayers read in the church ... The Sisters who taught in the poor school went to their duties ... The school lasted till twelve, when we went home and said Sext. We had dinner at twenty minutes to one, still in silence. The food was plain, good, and sufficient. After dinner we talked together in the Common Room. At three we said None ... The school was dismissed for the day at half-past four. At five there were three quarters of an hour for spiritual reading, then Vespers. Supper followed at six o'clock, and after it a few moments' ... relaxation. We then prepared for church: ... those who could not go after the fatigues of the day read the service at home. On our return from church at eight o'clock Compline was said, and the Sisters remained in the Oratory after its conclusion for private devotion till twenty minutes past nine, when Mattins was said. (Rowell, 1983, p. 94)

All of this shows yet another principle of Catholic mission: that laity (and later some clergy) are also to play a leading role, combining committed service of those in need, in a variety of ways, with a rule of life or monastic pattern of daily prayer and community finely tuned to the circumstances in which they live. The precise details of this combination would vary significantly from community to community, but the principle of combining prayer with what Anglicans now call the Third Mark of Mission, responding to human need with loving service, would be a constant foundation of this second great initiative of Tractarianism.

The Park Village community later joined another community of sisters at Devonport in the diocese of Exeter, where they became the Society of the Holy Trinity. Their superior, Lydia Sellon, recognized the importance of contemplative prayer within the life of the community and arranged for some sisters to have this as their primary vocation, a variation on the initial pattern. Pusey regarded Miss Sellon as 'the restorer after three centuries of the Religious Life in the English Church'. Rowell comments that 'there can be little doubt that what lay behind this was both Miss Sellon's organizing genius and the trust that grew between her and Pusey through difficult years' (Rowell, 1983, p. 95).

From the mid-century onwards a number of other female communities were founded, each one subtly altering the mix of service of those in need with monastic patterns of prayer. The most famous were probably the Wantage Sisters, founded in 1848, and the Community of St Margaret founded at East Grinstead in 1855 by John Mason Neale. The East Grinstead sisters were unusual because they served the rural poor rather than the urban poor. Also, a community of deaconesses was founded by Elizabeth Ferard in 1861, finding a home in the Notting Hill area of West London and serving those in need. In 1907 another development took place with the founding of the first enclosed or contemplative order for women, the Sisters of the Love of God at Fairacres in Oxford, shifting the emphasis wholly to monastic prayer. At about the same time another community, the Sisters of the Community of the Holy Comforter, also decided to become contemplatives and eventually moved to Malling Abbey in Kent. In the twentieth century, Franciscan sisters created a contemplative community at Freeland in Oxfordshire.

All of this shows adaptability and flexibility in this adventurous form of mission. For men the development of religious communities was slower. When Newman left Oxford and moved to Littlemore in 1841 he lived a community life with some companions, but there were no vows. Some of the Anglo-Catholic slum priests lived in a similar way in their vicarages, but again vows were not taken. But in the last part of the nineteenth century and early twentieth century some male communities were established, the first being the Cowley Fathers, who included priests as well as lay people. Richard Benson, who was vicar of Cowley, then a village about two miles from Oxford, was the pioneer in 1865. He founded a community named the Society of St John the Evangelist and the brethren quickly became known as the Cowley Fathers. It was established to combine a life of prayer under monastic vows with missionary and educational work, again illustrating the foundational principle of this form of mission. Its profound commitment to mission, an emphasis often forgotten in recent accounts of the revival (as indeed of the Catholic movement as a whole), is shown in the way it called itself a 'Society of Mission Priests'. The Society grew quickly and established separate congregations in the USA, with houses at Cambridge and Boston, Massachusetts, and also in Canada, with a house at Bracebridge in Ontario. These developments illustrate how Catholic mission was spreading far beyond the Church of England into other provinces of the Anglican Communion (see further James, 2019).

This last point is also illustrated by another male religious community founded by Charles Gore in 1892 when he was principal of Pusey House in Oxford. After Pusey's death in 1882 Gore had become the widely acknowledged leader of the movement. He gathered a small group of men together and they named the new venture the Community of the Resurrection. The following year when he became vicar of Radley in Oxfordshire the community moved to the vicarage there, and then in 1898 to Mirfield in West Yorkshire where it could be in closer contact with the industrial population of the north of England. Gore's vision was for a community that was adapted to the changed circumstances of the modern age. The pattern of community life was more open and flexible than in other communities, though from 1902 when Walter Frere was Superior he steered it towards a more conventional monastic pattern. (Gore found he was unable to live with the brethren and in 1894 moved to Westminster to become a canon at the Abbey.)

The Community of the Resurrection, in keeping with the academic interests of its founder, combined the monastic life with educational and scholarly work, another variation in this form of Catholic mission. A theological college for working-class ordinands was opened in the old stables of the house at Mirfield and quickly established itself as a major source of Anglo-Catholic clergy for the Church of England. Brethren also travelled to South Africa and what is now Zimbabwe (then Rhodesia) and opened secondary schools and a theological college, which have educated and trained future leaders of post-independent Zimbabwe and South Africa, both in the state and Church (later alumni including Archbishop Desmond Tutu, the scourge of apartheid and Nobel Peace Prize laureate). One of the most famous of the brethren was Trevor Huddleston, who while rector of Sophiatown in postwar Johannesburg became a prophetic agent of resistance against the apartheid regime, and author of the bestselling *Naught for Your Comfort*, which in the 1950s alerted the public in Britain and further afield to the profound injustice of the apartheid regime in South Africa and its appalling structures of separation between the races (see Wilkinson, 1992). All of this points to a seventh and very important principle of Catholic mission: that it includes protest against and struggle to transform unjust structures in society, fighting violence and bringing reconciliation between different peoples: all this expressing what is now called the Fourth Mark of Mission.

IV

This survey has revealed the missionary orientation of the Tractarians and those who followed them. Pickering describes Anglo-Catholicism as 'a missionary movement':

> What at first seems a strange fact about Anglo-Catholicism is that, despite its strong anti-Protestant stance, notions of mission and conversion were very much part of the movement ... For Anglo-Catholics and Evangelicals ... religion was something to wax enthusiastic about ... to be religious meant swimming against the stream: it certainly was not sitting at ease in Zion. Their task was to convert Anglicans themselves and make them take up positions where religion was an either/or way of life. Either one should be sincerely and devoutly religious or else abandon religion altogether. (Pickering, 2008, p. 65)

What, then, were the characteristics of this Catholic mission? This survey has highlighted seven principles that can now be collected together and summarized as a whole. We can also ask how these principles might find expression today.

- It is born and given energy by sharp anger and protest at the secularizing pressures of modern society, pressures that have cut people off from their connectedness with God and his Church; this protest finds expression in a determination to regain awareness and confidence in Christ's presence in the Church, a presence tangibly handed down through apostolic succession.
- Its paradigmatic expression is through a self-sacrificial ministry with those in need, one that does not just respond to immediate need but takes a proactive approach to addressing causes of poverty.
- It is not only about ministry to those in need but also, ultimately, the incorporation of all people into the society of the Church, a society of equals with divine authority deriving from God incarnate, one who unites divinity and humanity in his own person.
- It finds engaging ways of communicating with the people it is seeking to reach using multi-sensory forms of sacramental worship that enrich and supplement the written and spoken word.
- It is strengthened by the dialectic of conflict with those who would repress it: a costly engagement.
- Laity (and some clergy) are also to play a leading role, combining committed service of those in need, in a variety of ways, with a rule of life or monastic pattern of daily prayer and community finely tuned to the circumstances in which they live.
- It includes protest against and struggle to transform unjust structures in society, fighting violence and bringing reconciliation between different peoples: all this expressing what is now called the Fourth Mark of Mission.

When these principles are collected together in this way it becomes possible to begin to envisage how they might find expression today. For example, it is clear that they show that Anglo-Catholic churches that concentrate on providing liturgical worship alone are very far from embodying Catholic mission. From Keble onwards the engagement with and service of the people of the community beyond the congregation, and especially those most in need, has been central to the whole missionary enterprise. Catholic mission is not just about the Second Mark of Mission, important as this is. Furthermore, the hard edge of Catholic mission, resisting wilful opposition, at great cost to those leading the way, has been seen clearly in the late-nineteenth-century history of the movement, and this needs recovering. Finally, the importance of personal commitment to a rule of life – and, for some, to a publicly professed monastic pattern of daily prayer – will also need to play a central part in the movement.

But how and where might these principles find full and rich expression within the mission of Anglicanism today? This is a question for every Anglican who identifies with the Catholic movement: it demands some new, creative and radical answers.

Bibliography

Chadwick, Owen (1960), *The Mind of the Oxford Movement*, London: A & C Black.

Chadwick, Owen (1971), *The Victorian Church*, Volume 1, third edn, London: SCM Press.

Chandler, Michael (2003), *An Introduction to the Oxford Movement*, London: SPCK.

Herring, George (2002), *What Was the Oxford Movement?*, London: Continuum.

Hylson-Smith, Kenneth (1998), *The Churches in England from Elizabeth I to Elizabeth II, Vol. III*, London: SCM Press.

James, Serenhedd (2019), *The Cowley Fathers: A History of the English Congregation of the Society of St John the Evangelist*, Norwich: Canterbury Press.

Milbank, A. (2009), *Chesterton and Tolkien as Theologians*, London: T & T Clark.

Newman, John Henry (1833), *Tract 1*, online at www.newmanreader. org/works/times/tract1.html.

Nockles, Peter (1994), *The Oxford Movement in Context: Anglican High Churchmanship 1760–1867*, Cambridge: Cambridge University Press.

Pickering, W. S. F. (2008), *Anglo-Catholicism: A Study in Religious Ambiguity*, second edn, Cambridge: James Clarke and Co.

Rowell, Geoffrey (1983), *The Vision Glorious: Themes and Personalities of the Catholic Revival in Anglicanism*, Oxford: Oxford University Press.

Skinner, S. A. (2004), *Tractarians and the 'Condition of England': The Social and Political Thought of the Oxford Movement*, Oxford: Clarendon Press.

Wilberforce, Robert Isaac (1846), *A Charge to the Clergy of the East Riding*, London: John Murray.

Wilberforce, Robert Isaac (1848), *The Doctrine of the Incarnation of Our Lord Jesus Christ in its Relation to Mankind and the Church*, London: John Murray.

Wilkinson, Alan (1992), *The Community of the Resurrection: A Centenary History*, London: SCM Press.

Yates, Nigel (2000), *Anglican Ritualism in Victorian Britain 1830–1910*, Oxford: Clarendon Press.

Index